THE
PRIMROSE BAKERY
BOOK

MARTHA SWIFT · LISA THOMAS

SQUARE PEG

Published by Square Peg 2011

2 4 6 8 10 9 7 5 3 1

First published in Great Britain in 2011 by
Square Peg
Random House
20 Vauxhall Bridge Road
London SW1V 2SA

www.rbooks.co.uk

Addresses for companies within The Random House Group Limited can be found at: www.randomhouse.co.uk/offices.htm

The Random House Group Limited Reg. No. 954009

A CIP catalogue record for this book is available from the British Library

ISBN 9780224086882

Photography: Yuki Sugiura
Illustrations: Michael Heath
Design: Friederike Huber
Styling: Martha Swift & Lisa Thomas
Food styling: Valerie Berry

FSC
www.fsc.org
MIX
Paper from responsible sources
FSC™ C004592

The Random House Group Limited supports The Forest Stewardship Council (FSC), the leading international forest certification organisation. All our titles that are printed on Greenpeace approved FSC certified paper carry the FSC logo. Our paper procurement policy can be found at www.rbooks.co.uk/environment

Printed and bound in Germany Firmengruppe APPL, aprinta druck, Wemding

For our mothers, Caroline and Marlene

CONTENTS

INTRODUCTION

It's now seven years since we started Primrose Bakery in Lisa's home kitchen in Primrose Hill, North London. In October 2004 we decided that as we were not able to find the cakes and cupcakes that seemed to be so readily available elsewhere in the world, we would set up our own business. We had no five-year business plan, no professional background in cooking and no outside investment. We did, however, have a passion for baking and a huge desire to start a business of our own. We wanted to create a proper old-fashioned cake shop, based on the principles of home baking and excellent customer service.

We now have two shops in London – one in Primrose Hill and the other in Covent Garden – and our first book, *Cupcakes from the Primrose Bakery*, was published in 2009. At times we can't believe that something we started at home with just the two of us has grown so much. It gives us a huge sense of satisfaction to see people queuing out into the street on a Saturday afternoon waiting to buy our cakes – there is no better feeling than this, to see that people really do want to buy and eat what we have made, and it makes all the long hours worthwhile.

Our first book was very much based on cupcakes – quite rightly, as these were what we started with and they still form such an important part of what we do today. People often ask us, 'What happens after cupcakes?' but cupcakes, in one form or another, have been around for many years before we began making them and we truly believe that they will be around for many years to come. Their versatility and adaptability, combined with their huge visual appeal, means there is a place for cupcakes at every conceivable occasion, from a simple family tea to a big wedding.

However, Primrose Bakery has always been about more than cupcakes. We make our own croissants by hand and have a huge range of layer cakes, biscuits, cake slices, and so on. We wanted to build a business that would be known for the high quality of the baked goods it produced and

its excellent customer service, to create a place where everybody felt welcome and that would appeal to all. To do this, we wanted to take inspiration from the best we had seen and tasted in the US, Australia, Italy and France and create our own cake shop. Both our shops are painted in colours of yellow, mint green and pink, to tie in with the colours of many of our cakes and also to provide a warm, welcoming environment in which to enjoy eating them while escaping the often grey English light.

Therefore, we hope this book will represent our baking and our business as a whole. We still work to the same principles we started out with – to keep as close as possible to how we bake in a home kitchen while actually cooking on a professional level. We use equipment found in many domestic kitchens – electric hand mixers, food processors, spatulas, mixing bowls – and make everything in small batches, using very simple, high-quality, carefully sourced seasonal ingredients, with no artificial additives or preservatives. We ice all our cupcakes, cakes and biscuits by hand and bake every day – seven days a week, almost 365 days a year – so that everything we sell in our shops is freshly baked and to

ensure as little wastage as possible.

It's hard work, though. Even in our kitchens, where we bake the same sort of things every day, stuff goes wrong. Baking can be very temperamental: oven temperatures vary, cakes don't rise, they rise too much, tins are overfilled, cakes fall apart, cupcakes come out of their wrappers. Then, of course, there are the many other disasters – the first year we were open in Primrose Hill we lost our electricity supply for 24 hours in the run-up to Christmas; the cupcake cases we liked to use are no longer made by the manufacturer; we have run out of icing sugar, butter and, at one time or another, every ingredient we use; cakes have been dropped just as they are to be handed to a customer; the volcanic ash cloud in April 2010 meant we couldn't receive our supplies of decorations from abroad. The list is endless . . .

We hope that you find these recipes straightforward and easy to use. Of course we have added more cupcakes, as we are always developing new flavours, and this is the great thing about cupcakes – there really is no end to the possibilities of what you could do with them. We've also included many of our layer cakes, loaves, biscuits and croissants and hope that this

 **INTRODUCTION**

book gives a picture of what life is like in our shops on a daily basis and to encourage people to give it a go. We want to show how much pleasure can be gained from baking, both for the baker and the recipient.

We are now lucky enough to employ about 20 staff to help us prepare and sell our cakes in our shops. Since we began, we have employed so many interesting and varied people who have contributed greatly to Primrose Bakery and taught us so much. It is like having an extended family to add to our own families. Our own children (Martha's two daughters and Lisa's two sons) have grown up considerably in the last seven years and Martha's eldest daughter, Daisy, and Lisa's son Thomas (both 16) now work in the shops on the occasional weekend and in the school holidays. Martha's younger daughter, Millie, is already a fantastic cake icer at 13 and Lisa's younger son, Ned, who is 10, makes his own lemonade to sell on a stall outside in the summer. We've also had the privilege of working with some amazing companies and other people in the food industry, such as Miller Harris, Anya Hindmarch, Smythson, The Royal Ballet, Cath Kidston, DKNY and Mama Mio and

have catered for some fantastic events such as Vogue's Fashion Night Out, the Help for Heroes concert, the Capital Radio summertime and Jingle Bell balls, the Royal Variety Performance, the Museum of Everything launch, and many more.

One single problem with the cakes we produce in our shops is that they are slightly too fragile to transport far and, although we often travel to different venues all over the south-east of England to set up wedding cake tiers ourselves, on the whole we cannot supply cakes outside London. By publishing this book we can help the cakes reach a wider audience and hope that these recipes will inspire you to make your own and to try out different decorations and ingredients depending on what is available where you live. We have been amazed by the kind emails that people have sent to us since our first book was published and we want to show that all our recipes are achievable by everyone and that anything is possible.

Martha Swift and Lisa Thomas

 **INTRODUCTION**

CUPCAKES

Here you will find a selection of the new cupcakes we have developed over the last year or so and which we now sell regularly. We always enjoy trying out new possibilities, some of which work and some of which don't! A few of the recipes use sponges that may be familiar to you but we have combined them with interesting new icing flavours (and vice versa). You can also play around yourself, matching your favourite icings and sponges to create new flavours.

We like to vary the flavours of cupcakes at different times of year, depending on what fruit is in season. Using fresh seasonal fruit always ensures the best possible taste.

It would be impossible to exhaust the different kinds of cupcakes you could make and each has a visual and taste appeal of its own. This is why it's highly unlikely that cupcakes will ever decrease in popularity, as they fit in anywhere.

Unless otherwise stated, all these cupcakes can be kept in airtight containers and stored at room temperature for 2–3 days.

If you love perfumed flavours, then you will love our violet cupcakes – and not just the end result, because your senses will be treated from start to finish with the violet-drenched aroma of the syrup as you cook it and also the intense floral taste of the crystallised violet petals that we use to decorate the cakes at the end. Giving these cupcakes to someone would be as lovely as presenting them with a bunch of real violets!

VIOLET CUPCAKES

FOR THE VIOLET CUPCAKES

110g unsalted butter, at room temperature
225g golden caster sugar
2 large eggs, preferably free-range or organic
120ml semi-skimmed milk
1½ tbsp violet syrup
150g self-raising flour
125g plain flour

FOR THE TOPPING

1 batch Violet Buttercream Icing (see recipe overleaf)
Crystallised violet petals, to decorate

Makes 12 regular cupcakes

Note: we use Jardin d'Elan Sirop à la Violette, from La Fromagerie in London. It is expensive and can be tricky to get hold of but makes for a special treat. Other brands are available online (see Stockists on page 230).

Preheat the oven to 180°C/gas mark 4. Line a 12-hole muffin tray with muffin cases.

Cream the butter and sugar in a bowl, using an electric hand mixer, until the mixture is pale and smooth. Add the eggs, one at a time, mixing briefly after each addition – this can take a few minutes. Scrape down the sides of the bowl with a rubber spatula to ensure the mixture stays well combined.

Measure the milk into a plastic measuring jug and stir in the violet syrup. Sift the flours into a separate bowl and stir together.

Add one-third of the flour mix to the creamed butter and sugar mixture and beat well. Pour in one-third of the violet-flavoured milk and beat again. Repeat these steps until all the flour and milk/syrup has been added. You will notice that the batter will turn a grey/violet colour as the syrup is added. This is completely normal and, in fact, makes an interesting lilac coloured sponge cupcake once cooked.

Spoon the batter evenly into the muffin cases, filling them to about two-thirds full. Bake in the centre of the oven for about 25 minutes, until slightly raised and golden brown. To test if the cupcakes are cooked, insert a skewer into the centre of one of the cakes – it should come out clean.

Leave the cupcakes to cool in their tin for about 10 minutes before turning out onto a wire rack. Once completely cool, ice each one with the violet buttercream and decorate with the crystallised violet petals.

VIOLET BUTTERCREAM ICING

**115g unsalted butter, at room
  temperature**
60ml semi-skimmed milk
1 tsp good-quality vanilla extract
500g icing sugar, sifted
1–2 tbsp violet syrup, or to taste

Makes enough to ice 12 regular cupcakes

In a bowl beat together the butter, milk, vanilla extract
and half the icing sugar until smooth, using an electric
hand mixer. This will usually take a few minutes.

Gradually beat in the remainder of the icing sugar to
produce a buttercream with a creamy and smooth
consistency. Add a little of the violet syrup and beat
well. Continue to add more syrup until the desired
taste and colour are reached – the syrup will also turn
the icing a beautiful lilac shade so you will not need to
add any food colouring.

Store in an airtight container at room temperature
for up to 3 days. Beat well again before reusing.

 **CUPCAKES**

 **CUPCAKES**

After the success of our Malted Marshmallow Cupcakes, we decided to experiment more and devised these Cookies and Cream ones as well as the Chocolate and Marshmallow Cupcakes on page 24. Although not as subtle a cupcake as we normally make, they go down particularly well with children.

COOKIES AND CREAM CUPCAKES

FOR THE CHOCOLATE CUPCAKES

115g good-quality dark chocolate
(at least 70% cocoa solids)
85g unsalted butter, at room temperature
175g soft brown sugar
2 large eggs, free-range or organic,
separated
185g plain flour
¾ tsp baking powder
¾ tsp bicarbonate of soda
Pinch of salt
250ml semi-skimmed milk, at room
temperature
1 tsp good-quality vanilla extract

FOR THE TOPPING

1 batch Marshmallow Icing (see recipe
overleaf)
1 packet Oreo cookies, crushed or
broken into small pieces, to decorate

Makes 16 regular cupcakes

Preheat the oven to 190°C/gas mark 5.
Line 2 x 12-hole muffin trays with 16 muffin cases.

Melt the chocolate: you can do this in a heatproof bowl set over a saucepan of simmering water on the hob, but the easiest way is in the microwave – place the chocolate in a microsafe bowl and heat on a medium heat for 1 minute, stir and then microwave again for a further minute – but be very careful not to burn the chocolate. Leave to cool slightly.

In a bowl cream the butter and sugar together, using an electric hand mixer, until pale and smooth. Slowly add the egg yolks and beat well. Next, add the melted chocolate and beat well again.

Sift the flour, baking powder, bicarbonate of soda and salt into a separate bowl and stir together. Measure the milk into a jug and stir in the vanilla extract. Gradually add alternate amounts of the flour mixture and the milk to the chocolate, butter and sugar mixture, beating well after each addition.

In a clean bowl and using a clean whisk, whisk the egg whites until stiff peaks have formed. Then, using a spatula, carefully fold the eggs whites into the main batter until it is all combined.

Spoon the mixture equally into the muffin cases, filling them to about two-thirds full. Bake for 20–25 minutes. Leave the cupcakes to cool in their tin for about 10 minutes before turning them out onto a wire rack to cool completely.

Ice them with the marshmallow icing and decorate with some of the broken Oreo pieces.

 **CUPCAKES**

MARSHMALLOW ICING

120g granulated sugar
80g golden syrup
1½ tbsp water
2 large egg whites
½ tsp good-quality vanilla extract
  (optional)

Makes enough to ice 16 regular cupcakes
with some left over

Place the sugar, golden syrup and water into a sauce-pan or a shallow frying pan and cook on a high heat until the mixture reaches the soft-ball stage – this is when the bubbles in the mixture almost start to stick together and would drop off a spoon in a smooth, slow stream. This could take about 2 minutes on a high heat. When it reaches this stage, remove from the heat.

In the bowl of a freestanding mixer or a food processor, whisk the egg whites until soft peaks start to form. Now, with the machine on a low speed, slowly and evenly pour the hot sugar mixture into the bowl. Continue to beat on a low speed until all the hot sugar is in the mixing bowl.

Increase the speed to medium-high and continue whipping until the mixture becomes thick, glossy and cool. Add the vanilla extract, if using, towards the end of the mixing process.

This icing is easiest to work with while it is still a little warm, so try to use it right away. If you have some left over, store it in the fridge overnight, but we would not recommend keeping any unused icing for longer than that. You will need to beat it again gently with a spoon or spatula if using straight from the fridge.

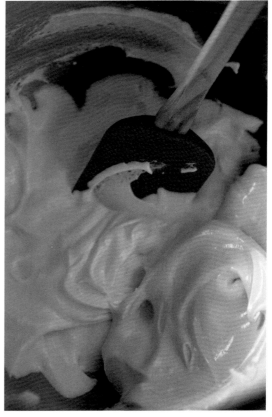

  **CUPCAKES**

This is a simple variation on the Cookies and Cream Cupcakes on page 21. You will need some pink food colouring, a packet of marshmallows and some edible glitter.

CHOCOLATE AND MARSHMALLOW CUPCAKES

1 batch Chocolate Cupcakes
  (see recipe for Cookies and Cream
  Cupcakes on page 21)

FOR THE TOPPING
1 batch Marshmallow Icing
  (see recipe on previous page)
Pink food colouring
1 packet marshmallows
Edible glitter, to decorate

Make up the chocolate cupcakes and the marshmallow icing. Once you have made the icing, add a few drops of pink colouring to it and beat again. Keep adding the colouring until you reach your desired shade of pink. Spread each cupcake with the marshmallow icing and then place a marshmallow on top of each cake and sprinkle with edible glitter.

These cupcakes are best eaten on the same day they are made.

Makes 16 regular cupcakes

 **CUPCAKES**

These cupcakes were developed by us for *InStyle* magazine and are a cupcake version of a lime meringue pie. The slightly sour citrus taste of the lime goes very well with the sweet meringue on the top and really has no need for any other decoration.

FRESH LIME MERINGUE CUPCAKES

FOR THE LIME CUPCAKES

110g unsalted butter, at room temperature

225g golden caster sugar

2 large eggs, free-range or organic

90ml semi-skimmed milk

30ml freshly squeezed lime juice

1 tbsp sour cream

150g self-raising flour

125g plain flour

1 tsp (roughly 2 limes' worth) grated lime zest

FOR THE TOPPING

Approx. 12 tsp lime curd (lime marmalade would work well too)

1 batch Meringue Icing (see recipe overleaf)

Grated lime zest, to decorate (optional)

Makes 12 regular cupcakes

Preheat the oven to 180°C/gas mark 4. Line a 12-hole muffin tray with muffin cases.

In a large bowl cream the butter and sugar together, using an electric hand mixer, until light and fluffy. Add the eggs, one at a time, and beat well after each addition.

Measure the milk into a jug, add the lime juice and sour cream and combine well. Sift the flours into a bowl and stir together.

Add alternate amounts of the flour and the lime-flavoured milk to the creamed butter and sugar as follows: add one-third of the flour and mix well; add half the milk and mix well; add another third of flour and mix well; add the remainder of the milk and mix well; finish by adding the last third of flour and then the lime zest, and beat well. If the mixture looks as though it is curdling slightly, don't panic – simply add another spoonful of plain flour and beat well.

Spoon the mixture evenly into the muffin cases, filling them to about two-thirds full. Bake in the centre of the oven for 25 minutes. To test if the cupcakes are cooked, insert a skewer into the centre of one of the cakes – it should come out clean. The cupcakes will appear quite a light golden brown colour even when cooked.

Leave the cupcakes to cool slightly in their tin for 10 minutes and then carefully turn them out onto a wire rack to cool completely. Once the cupcakes are out of the oven, reduce the oven temperature to 160°C/gas mark 3, ready for finishing the iced cupcakes later.

When the cupcakes are completely cool, cut a small hole in the top of each cake and discard (or eat!), then, using a sharp knife or a teaspoon, carefully place 1 teaspoon of lime curd inside the sponge.

To ice the cakes, use a piping bag or a tablespoon to pipe or spoon the Meringue Icing over the surface of each cake, covering it completely. Put the cupcakes on a lined baking tray and return them to the oven for about 15 minutes, until the meringue has set slightly and has a slight golden tinge.

Let the cupcakes cool again before serving. You could grate a small amount of lime zest over the finished cupcakes if you wanted.

 **CUPCAKES**

MERINGUE ICING

4 large egg whites
225g golden caster sugar

Makes enough to ice 12 regular cupcakes
and 36 mini cupcakes

In a clean bowl beat the egg whites with an electric
hand mixer until stiff peaks form. Add 1 tablespoon of
the caster sugar and beat well until incorporated. Add
the remaining sugar and beat well again until the
mixture takes on a glossy sheen. Use straight away.

 CUPCAKES

A simple variation on the Fresh Lime Meringue Cupcakes on page 26, these mini cupcakes are always a bestseller at the Miller Harris tearoom in Mayfair, London. They are the perfect complement to the amazing range of fragrant teas designed by Lyn Harris, and both can be enjoyed while gazing at the beautiful perfumes and bath and beauty products in the shop in front.

LEMON MERINGUE MINI CUPCAKES

**1 batch lemon cupcakes
(see method on right)
1 batch Meringue Icing
(see recipe on previous page)**

Makes 36 mini cupcakes

Line 3 x 12-hole mini muffin trays with mini muffin cases.

To make the cupcakes, follow the instructions for making the batter in the recipe for Fresh Lime Meringue Cupcakes on page 26 but substitute the lime juice and zest with the same amount of lemon juice and zest and use lemon curd instead of lime curd.

Spoon the mixture into the mini muffin cases and bake for 13 minutes or so, until risen and golden brown. Allow to cool fully, before inserting the lemon curd into each cake then piping or spreading with the Meringue Icing and returning to the oven, as described on page 27. However, these mini cupcakes will need only about 10 minutes in the oven for the icing to set slightly.

As with the Fresh Lime Meringue Cupcakes, these are best eaten on the day they are made.

 **CUPCAKES**

Summer brings fresh raspberries to our kitchens. As each season changes and new fruit arrives, we always experiment to make something entirely new. Everyone in the kitchen gets involved and comes up with ideas, so it is definitely one part of our work we really love – unlike paying the bills! This recipe came about when we were asked by the *Sunday Times* 'Style' magazine to create a cupcake that would be fitting at an English picnic. A theme of English gardens and summer fairgrounds was agreed on and this came together for us in the cupcake below, with its pink and white swirl.

RASPBERRY COCONUT ICE CUPCAKES

FOR THE RASPBERRY CUPCAKES
225g golden caster sugar
1 tsp baking powder
210g self-raising flour, sifted
25g cornflour
225g unsalted butter
4 large eggs, free-range or organic
150g crushed fresh raspberries

FOR THE TOPPING
Approx. 12 tsp good-quality
  raspberry jam
Coconut Buttercream Icing
 (see recipe overleaf)
Fresh raspberries, to decorate

Makes 12 regular cupcakes

Preheat the oven to 180°C/gas mark 4. Line a 12-hole muffin tray with muffin cases.

Put the sugar, baking powder, flour and cornflour into a food processor. Pulse until evenly mixed (about 4 seconds). Add the remaining ingredients, except for the crushed raspberries, and process briefly until evenly mixed (about 10 seconds). If you prefer to use an electric hand mixer, cream the butter and sugar together first, beat in the eggs one by one, and then add the remaining ingredients and beat well together. Add the crushed raspberries and mix through the batter gently by hand.

Divide the mixture evenly between the muffin cases, filling them to about two-thirds full. Bake in the centre of the oven for 25 minutes, or until cooked and a skewer inserted into the centre of one of the cakes comes out clean. The cakes will appear fairly moist even when cooked.

Allow the cakes to cool in their tin for 10 minutes before carefully turning out onto a wire rack.

Once the cakes are completely cool, carefully make a small hole in the centre of each cupcake with a sharp knife or a teaspoon (you can discard or eat the cut-out sponge) and place a small amount (about a teaspoonful) of raspberry jam inside the sponge.

To finish the cupcakes, ice one side of each with the pink Coconut Buttercream and the other side with the uncoloured Coconut Buttercream. Using a palette knife or flat-edged knife, swirl the icings together in the centre. Finish with several fresh raspberries.

 **CUPCAKES**

  CUPCAKES

COCONUT BUTTERCREAM ICING

**115g unsalted butter, at room
  temperature**
60ml coconut milk
1 tsp good-quality vanilla extract
500g icing sugar, sifted
75g desiccated coconut
A few drops pink food colouring

Makes enough to ice 12 regular cupcakes

In a bowl beat the butter, milk, vanilla extract and half the icing sugar with an electric hand mixer until smooth. This will usually take a few minutes. Gradually add the remainder of the icing sugar to produce a buttercream with a creamy and smooth consistency. Beat in the desiccated coconut.

If using to ice the Raspberry Coconut Ice Cupcakes, divide the mixture between 2 bowls. Add a few drops of pink colouring to one of the bowls and beat well. Leave the icing in the second bowl uncoloured.

The buttercream can be stored in an airtight container for up to 3 days at room temperature. Before reusing beat well.

Serious chocolate lovers – and probably most children – will adore these rich cupcakes, and they won't fail to satisfy on those occasions when only something chocolatey will do.

TRIPLE CHOCOLATE CUPCAKES

**1 batch chocolate cupcakes
(see recipe for Cookies and Cream
Cupcakes on page 21)**
**1 batch Milk Chocolate Icing
(see recipe opposite)**
**1 standard-size (100g) bar white
chocolate, grated, or 1 packet white
chocolate buttons, to decorate**

Make the cupcakes and, once they have cooled, ice each one with a good spoonful of the Milk Chocolate Icing and then decorate with a sprinkling of grated white chocolate or several white chocolate buttons.

Makes 16 regular cupcakes

 **CUPCAKES**

MILK CHOCOLATE ICING

**300g good-quality milk chocolate
(at least 20% cocoa solids), broken
into small pieces**
60ml double cream
**2 tbsp unsalted butter, at room
temperature**
½ tsp good-quality vanilla extract

Makes enough to ice 16 regular cupcakes

Melt the chocolate either in a heatproof bowl over
a saucepan of simmering water on the hob, or in a
microsafe bowl in the microwave (heat on a medium
heat for 1 minute, stir and then heat for a further
minute, taking care not to burn the chocolate). When
the chocolate is melted and runny pour into a mixing
bowl and leave to sit.

Once the chocolate has cooled a little, add the
cream, butter and vanilla extract and beat well with an
electric hand mixer until the mixture is smooth and
well combined.

The icing will probably need to go in the fridge for
about half an hour to set a little before using. You may
need to beat it once again before using. Any unused
icing should be stored in the fridge, where it will keep
for 3–4 days.

We usually make these cupcakes around Halloween and Christmas but you could make them at any time. We have slightly adapted our original recipe to make them a little moister and combined them with a white chocolate icing – these particular cupcakes were created for an event we did with Smythson, the stylish English leather goods company.

CRANBERRY AND ORANGE CUPCAKES

FOR THE CUPCAKES

3 large eggs, free-range or organic
200g golden caster sugar
90ml corn oil
125g sour cream
1 tsp grated orange zest
1 tsp good-quality vanilla extract
230g plain flour
½ tsp baking powder
¼ tsp bicarbonate of soda
¼ tsp salt
1 tsp ground cinnamon
140g dried cranberries, chopped into
** small pieces**

FOR THE TOPPING

1 batch White Chocolate Icing
** (see recipe overleaf)**
A few cranberries, to decorate,
** either dried or fresh (optional)**

Makes 12 regular cupcakes or
36 mini cupcakes

Preheat the oven to 180°C/gas mark 4. Line a 12-hole muffin tray or 3 x 12-hole mini muffin trays with the appropriate size muffin cases.

In a bowl beat the eggs and sugar together, using an electric hand mixer. Slowly pour in the oil, beating well after each addition, and then repeat the process with the sour cream, orange zest and vanilla extract, making sure everything is well combined.

Sift all the dry ingredients together in a bowl and then add to the liquid mixture and beat well. Finally, fold in the cranberries.

Divide the mixture evenly between the muffin cases and bake in the centre of the oven for about 20-25 minutes for the regular size and 17 minutes for the mini ones, until risen and golden. To test if the cupcakes are cooked, insert a skewer into the centre of one of the cakes – it should come out clean.

Allow the cupcakes to cool in their tin (or tins) for 10 minutes or so before turning them out onto a wire rack. When the cupcakes are completely cool, ice each one with the White Chocolate Icing and decorate with a few cranberries.

 CUPCAKES

WHITE CHOCOLATE ICING

200g good-quality white chocolate
Approx. 120g (8 tbsp) Vanilla
  Buttercream Icing (see recipe on
  page 52)
6 tbsp double cream

Makes enough to ice 12 regular cupcakes
or 36 mini cupcakes

Melt the chocolate either in a heatproof bowl over a
saucepan of simmering water on the hob, or in a
microsafe bowl in the microwave (heat on a medium
heat for 1 minute, stir and then heat for a further
minute, taking care not to burn the chocolate). When
the chocolate is melted and runny pour into a large
mixing bowl and leave to sit.

When the chocolate has cooled a little, add the
vanilla buttercream and the double cream and beat
well with an electric hand mixer until it all comes
together. The icing is usually too runny to use immediately so would benefit from being put in the fridge for
a little while to thicken up. If it does begin to stiffen
too much, soften it with a bit more double cream or
place in the microwave for 10 seconds, then beat well
again before using.

This icing needs to be stored in the fridge because it
contains cream. It will keep well in the fridge for at
least a week. You will need to bring it to room
temperature and beat well again if using straight from
the fridge.

A great alternative to a mince pie or a Christmas pudding, these cupcakes are delicious iced with Brandy Buttercream and decorated with holly and berries.

CHRISTMAS PUDDING CUPCAKES

FOR THE CHRISTMAS PUDDING CUPCAKES
225g unsalted butter
225g golden caster sugar
4 large eggs, free-range or organic
210g self-raising flour
25g cornflour
250g good-quality mincemeat
1 tsp baking powder

FOR THE TOPPING
1 batch Brandy Buttercream Icing
  (see recipe opposite)
Sprigs of holly and fresh berries,
  to decorate (optional)

Makes 12 regular cupcakes

Preheat the oven to 180°C/gas mark 4. Line a 12-hole muffin tray with muffin cases.

Using an electric hand mixer, cream the butter and sugar together in a bowl until light and fluffy, then beat in the eggs, one by one. Add the remaining ingredients and beat well together.

Divide the mixture evenly between the muffin cases, filling them to about two-thirds full. Bake in the centre of the oven for 20–23 minutes, or until raised and quite a dark golden brown. When they are cooked, a skewer inserted into the centre of one of the cakes should come out clean. The cakes will appear fairly moist even when cooked.

Allow the cupcakes to cool in their tin for 10 minutes before turning out onto a wire rack. Once they are completely cool, spread each cake with the Brandy Buttercream Icing and decorate with sprigs of holly and fresh berries if desired.

BRANDY BUTTERCREAM ICING

**115g unsalted butter, at room
  temperature**
30ml semi-skimmed milk
1 tsp good-quality vanilla extract
30ml brandy
500g icing sugar, sifted

Makes enough to ice 12 regular cupcakes,
or you can double the quantities to ice a
20cm Christmas cake

Using an electric hand mixer, beat the butter, milk,
vanilla extract, brandy and half the icing sugar in a
bowl until smooth. This will usually take a few minutes. Gradually add the remainder of the icing sugar to
produce a buttercream with a creamy and smooth
consistency.

Taste the buttercream to check if there is enough
brandy, and add a little more if needed, although bear
in mind how strong it could end up being!

The buttercream can be stored in an airtight container at room temperature for up to 3 days. Beat well
again before reusing.

 **CUPCAKES**

We usually make these cupcakes in the autumn, after strawberries and raspberries have gone out of season. Try to use the best-quality jam you can find for the sponge and the ripest, sweetest fresh plums for decoration as this will make a real difference to the end result.

PLUM CUPCAKES

FOR THE PLUM CUPCAKES

112g unsalted butter, at room temperature
180g golden caster sugar
2 large eggs, free-range or organic
125ml semi-skimmed milk
½ tsp good-quality vanilla extract
125g self-raising flour
120g plain flour
4 tbsp good-quality plum jam

FOR THE TOPPING

1 batch Vanilla Buttercream Icing (see recipe overleaf)
2–3 fresh plums, to decorate

Makes 12 regular cupcakes

Preheat the oven to 180°C/gas mark 4. Line a 12-hole muffin tray with muffin cases.

Using an electric hand mixer, cream the butter and sugar in a bowl until the mixture is pale and smooth. Add the eggs, one at a time, mixing briefly after each addition. This can take a few minutes. Scrape down the sides of the bowl with a rubber spatula to ensure the mixture stays well combined.

Measure the milk into a plastic measuring jug and stir in the vanilla extract.

Sift the flours into a separate bowl and combine well.

Add one-third of the flour to the creamed butter and sugar and beat well. Pour in one-third of the milk and beat again. Repeat these steps until all the flour and milk has been added.

Gently fold in the plum jam until most of it is combined. It's OK to have some jam streaks running through the mixture.

Carefully spoon the batter evenly into the muffin cases, to about two-thirds full. Bake in the centre of the oven for about 25 minutes, until slightly raised and golden brown and a skewer inserted into the centre of one of the cakes comes out clean.

Leave the cupcakes to cool slightly in their tin for 10 minutes before turning out onto a wire rack.

Once the cupcakes are completely cool, ice each one with Vanilla Buttercream. Just before serving, finely slice the plums and decorate each cupcake with a few slices, arranging them in a fan-like pattern.

 **CUPCAKES**

VANILLA BUTTERCREAM ICING

115g unsalted butter, at room temperature
60ml semi-skimmed milk
1 tsp good-quality vanilla extract
500g icing sugar, sifted

Makes enough to ice 12 regular cupcakes

Using an electric hand mixer, beat the butter, milk, vanilla extract and half the icing sugar in a bowl until smooth. This will usually take a few minutes. Gradually add the remainder of the icing sugar to produce a buttercream with a creamy and smooth consistency.

The buttercream can be stored in an airtight container for up to 3 days at room temperature. Beat well again before reusing.

 **CUPCAKES**

At first we found that rhubarb was quite a tricky ingredient to add to a cupcake, but it is such a delicious fruit and such a pretty pink colour that we were determined to make it work. We hope you agree that we succeeded!

RHUBARB CUPCAKES

FOR THE STEWED RHUBARB
300g chopped rhubarb
3 tbsp granulated sugar
250ml water

FOR THE RHUBARB SPONGE
110g unsalted butter
225g golden caster sugar
2 large eggs, free-range or organic
150g self-raising flour
125g plain flour
1 tsp ground ginger
80ml milk
300g stewed rhubarb (from above)

FOR THE TOPPING
1 batch Rhubarb Buttercream Icing
  (see recipe opposite)

Makes 12 regular cupcakes

First, stew the rhubarb – you could do this in advance if you wanted. Put the rhubarb, sugar and water into a saucepan over a medium heat for about 5–7 minutes until the rhubarb starts to break up. Once this happens, strain the rhubarb juice into another pan and place over a high heat for another 5–7 minutes until it has reduced to about 50ml juice. The stewed rhubarb will be used in the cupcake sponge and the juice will be used in the icing.

Preheat the oven to 180°C/gas mark 4. Line a 12 hole muffin tray with muffin cases.

Cream the butter and sugar in a bowl with an electric hand mixer until light and fluffy. Beat in the eggs, one at a time, mixing briefly after each.

Sift the flours into a bowl, add the ginger and stir together. Add half of this mixture to the creamed butter and sugar and beat well. Add 40ml of the milk and beat again. Beat in the remaining flour and then the last 40ml of milk. Finally, fold in the stewed rhubarb with a spoon and combine well.

Divide the mixture evenly between the muffin cases, filling them to about two-thirds full. Bake in the centre of the oven for 25 minutes, until raised and golden brown and a skewer inserted into the centre of one of the cakes comes out clean. Allow the cupcakes to cool in their tins for 10 minutes and then turn out onto a wire rack to cool completely.

Ice each cupcake with a good spoonful of the rhubarb buttercream.

RHUBARB BUTTERCREAM ICING

**110g unsalted butter, at room
temperature**
500g icing sugar, sifted
**50ml rhubarb juice
(from recipe opposite)**

Makes enough to ice 12 regular cupcakes

In a bowl beat the butter and half the icing sugar with
an electric hand mixer until smooth. Add the rhubarb
juice and beat well. Slowly add the remaining icing
sugar until you have a creamy buttercream icing that
has a lovely pale pink hint to it from the rhubarb juice.
Keep any unused icing in an airtight container at room
temperature for 3–4 days.

When it became clear that we were firmly ensconced in the business of cupcakes, many of the new flavours we developed were inspired both by our own tastes and those of our children. This cupcake is one such recipe, as Lisa's son Ned and Martha's daughter Millie believe that Nutella should be eaten with everything. Although this fact is somewhat debatable, as a cupcake flavour it has proved to be an undeniable success!

NUTELLA CUPCAKES

FOR THE NUTELLA CUPCAKES

175g unsalted butter, at room temperature
175g golden caster sugar
3 large eggs, free-range or organic
200g self-raising flour, sifted
1 tsp baking powder
2 tsp ground cinnamon
4 tbsp milk
12 tsp Nutella chocolate hazelnut spread

FOR THE TOPPING
1 batch Milk Chocolate and Nutella Icing (see recipe opposite)

Makes 12 regular cupcakes

Preheat the oven to 180°C/gas mark 4. Line a 12-hole muffin tray with muffin cases.

In a bowl cream the butter and sugar with an electric hand mixer until the mixture is pale and smooth. Beat in the eggs, one at a time, mixing briefly after each addition. Gradually beat in the flour, baking powder and cinnamon and then the milk.

Heat the Nutella in a small pan on the hob until very slightly warm and easier to stir.

Divide the batter evenly between the muffin cases, to about two-thirds full. Spoon a teaspoonful of the warmed Nutella on top of each and gently swirl it through the batter with a skewer or small spoon.

Bake in the centre of the oven for 20–25 minutes, or until raised and golden brown and a skewer inserted into the centre of one of the cakes comes out clean. Allow the cupcakes to cool in their tin for 10 minutes before turning them out onto a wire rack.

When the cupcakes are completely cool, spread each one with a good spoonful of the Milk Chocolate and Nutella Icing and decorate as you wish – perhaps even with a Ferrero Rocher chocolate!

MILK CHOCOLATE AND NUTELLA ICING

**300g good-quality milk chocolate
 (at least 20% cocoa solids)
60ml double cream
2 tbsp unsalted butter
½ tsp good-quality vanilla extract
250g Nutella chocolate hazelnut spread**

Makes enough to ice 12 regular cupcakes

Melt the chocolate either in a heatproof bowl over a saucepan of simmering water on the hob, or in a microsafe bowl in the microwave (heat on a medium heat for 1 minute, stir and then heat for a further minute, taking care not to burn the chocolate). When the chocolate is melted and runny, pour into a large mixing bowl and allow to cool slightly.

Add the double cream, butter and vanilla extract and beat well with an electric hand mixer. Beat in the Nutella until the icing is smooth and creamy. It should be suitable to use straight away, but if it is a little runny put it into the fridge for half an hour or so. You can store any unused icing in the fridge for 3–4 days. Before reusing, allow it to come to room temperature and beat well.

 **CUPCAKES**

Our Earl Grey Cupcakes have been immensely popular so we thought it was time to produce another tea-flavoured cupcake.

GREEN TEA CUPCAKES

FOR THE GREEN TEA CUPCAKES

150ml semi-skimmed milk

4 green tea teabags

2½ tsp green tea (Matcha) powder

110g unsalted butter, at room temperature

225g granulated sugar

2 large eggs, free-range or organic

125g self-raising flour

120g plain flour

FOR THE TOPPING

1 batch Green Tea Buttercream Icing (see recipe overleaf)

A little green tea powder, to decorate

Makes 12 regular cupcakes

Heat the milk in a saucepan over a medium heat until it just begins to boil. Remove from the heat and add the teabags. Cover with clingfilm and let the mixture steep for at least 30 minutes, or longer if possible. You could even leave this overnight in the fridge.

When you are ready to make the cupcakes, preheat the oven to 180°C/gas mark 4. Line a 12-hole muffin tray with muffin cases.

Remove the teabags from the milk and squeeze out any excess milk into the pan. Add the green tea powder, and stir.

In a bowl cream the butter and sugar with an electric hand mixer until the mixture is pale and smooth. Add the eggs, one at a time, mixing briefly after each addition.

Sift the flours into a separate bowl and stir well.

Add one-third of the flour mix to the creamed butter and sugar and beat well. Pour in one-third of the milk/tea mixture and beat again. Repeat these steps until all the flour and milk has been added.

Carefully spoon the mixture evenly into the muffin cases, to about two-thirds full. Bake in the oven for about 25 minutes, until raised and golden brown. The cakes will have a greenish tinge to them.

Leave the cupcakes in their tin for 10 minutes or so before turning out onto a wire rack. When completely cool, ice with the Green Tea Buttercream Icing and sprinkle with a little green tea powder.

GREEN TEA BUTTERCREAM ICING

**115g unsalted butter, at room
 temperature**
60ml semi-skimmed milk
1 tsp good-quality vanilla extract
500g icing sugar, sifted
**Approx. 1 tsp green tea (Matcha)
 powder**

Makes enough to ice 12 regular cupcakes

Beat the butter, milk, vanilla extract and half the icing sugar until smooth. This will usually take a few minutes. Gradually add the remainder of the icing sugar and the green tea powder to produce a buttercream with a creamy and smooth consistency.

The green tea powder should be sufficient to achieve the desired green shade of icing so you won't need to add any food colouring.

The buttercream can be stored in an airtight container for up to 3 days at room temperature. Beat well again before reusing.

 **CUPCAKES**

These cupcakes were designed by Annice Curtis, winner of a competition we held on our Facebook page in aid of the Wellbeing of Women (WOW) charity. We sold the cupcakes in our shops to raise money for the charity and they have since become a firm favourite with our customers.

MAPLE AND PECAN CUPCAKES

FOR THE MAPLE AND PECAN CUPCAKES

115g unsalted butter, at room temperature
50g soft brown sugar
160ml maple syrup
2 large eggs, free-range or organic
115g self-raising flour, sifted
60g pecan nuts, roughly chopped

FOR THE CARAMELISED NUTS

60g golden caster sugar
20 pecan nut halves

FOR THE TOPPING

1 batch Maple Syrup Buttercream Icing (see recipe overleaf)

Makes 10 regular cupcakes

Preheat the oven to 180°C/gas mark 4. Line a 12-hole muffin tray with 10 muffin cases.

Using an electric mixer, cream the butter and the sugar together in a bowl until pale and smooth. Add the maple syrup and beat well. Add the eggs, one at a time, mixing briefly after each addition.

Using a spoon, fold the flour into the batter and beat well, then fold in the nuts.

Carefully spoon the mixture evenly into the muffin cases, filling each case to about two-thirds full. Bake in the centre of the oven for 20–25 minutes, until risen and golden and a skewer inserted into the centre of one of the cakes comes out clean. Leave the cupcakes to cool slightly in their tin for 10 minutes and then carefully turn out onto a wire rack to cool completely.

Meanwhile, make the caramelised pecans. Gently heat the caster sugar in a heavy-based saucepan until the sugar has melted and is a pale golden colour. Spread the nuts onto a sheet of baking paper, then pour the melted sugar over the nuts, covering them completely. Leave to sit. Once the caramel has cooled and hardenend, break into 20 pieces, ensuring there is a pecan half in each.

Ice the cupcakes with the Maple Syrup Buttercream, then top each cake with a caramelised pecan.

MAPLE SYRUP BUTTERCREAM ICING

**150g unsalted butter, at room
  temperature**
135ml maple syrup
435g icing sugar, sifted

Makes enough to ice 10 regular cupcakes

Using an electric hand mixer, beat the butter, maple syrup and half the icing sugar in a bowl until smooth. This will usually take a few minutes. Gradually add the remainder of the icing sugar to produce a buttercream with a creamy and smooth consistency.

The buttercream can be stored in an airtight container for up to 3 days at room temperature. Beat well again before reusing.

 **CUPCAKES**

 **CUPCAKES**

Our take on Black Forest gateau in cupcake form, but given that cherries and chocolate go so well together who could blame us?

CHERRY CHOCOLATE CUPCAKES

FOR THE CHERRY CHOCOLATE CUPCAKES

1 batch chocolate cupcake sponge batter (see recipe for Cookies and Cream Cupcakes on page 21)
230g dried cherries, chopped
Approx. 8 tsp cherry jam

FOR THE TOPPING

1 batch Vanilla Buttercream Icing (see recipe on page 52)
1 standard-sized (about 100g) bar good-quality plain chocolate (at least 70% cocoa solids), broken into small pieces
16 fresh cherries

Makes 16 regular cupcakes

Preheat the oven to 190°C/gas mark 5. Line 2 x 12-hole muffin tins with 16 muffin cases.

Make up the chocolate sponge batter, following the method for the Cookies and Cream Cupcakes on page 21 but once all the flour and milk has been added, stir in the dried cherries before whisking the egg whites and folding into the batter.

Spoon the mixture out evenly into the muffin cases, to about two-thirds full. Into each then add ½ teaspoon of cherry jam and carefully swirl it though the mixture. Bake in the centre of the oven for 20–25 minutes, until cooked and a skewer inserted into the centre of one of the cakes comes out clean.

Leave the cupcakes to cool slightly in their tins for 10 minutes and then carefully turn out onto a wire rack. While the cakes are cooling, make up the Vanilla Buttercream Icing as directed on page 52. Melt the chocolate either in a heatproof bowl over a pan of simmering water, stirring continually, or in a microsafe bowl in the microwave (heat on a medium heat for 1 minute, stir and then heat for a further minute, taking care not to burn the chocolate). When it is melted and runny, pour into a bowl and allow to cool slightly. Then dip each cherry into the chocolate and coat well. Place them on a sheet of baking paper and leave to set.

When everything is ready and the cakes are cool, ice each cupcake with vanilla buttercream and decorate with a chocolate cherry.

CUPCAKES

An excellent way of using up overripe bananas that are turning black and you might otherwise be tempted to throw away. The resulting cupcakes will be very soft and moist and could even be eaten without icing, as a banana muffin.

BANOFFEE PIE CUPCAKES

FOR THE BANOFFEE PIE CUPCAKES

125g unsalted butter, at room temperature
250g golden caster sugar
2 large eggs, free-range or organic, lightly beaten
1 tsp good-quality vanilla extract
250g plain flour, sifted
2 tsp baking powder
4 ripe bananas (preferably turning black), mashed with a fork or broken by hand into small pieces

FOR THE TOPPING

½ batch Caramel Buttercream Icing (see recipe on page 112)
1 packet dried banana chips, to decorate

Makes 12 regular cupcakes

Preheat the oven to 180°C/gas mark 4. Line a 12-hole muffin tray with muffin cases.

Cream the butter and sugar in a bowl with an electric hand mixer until the mixture is pale and smooth. Add the eggs, one at a time, mixing briefly after each addition. Add the vanilla extract and beat again briefly. Gradually add the flour and the baking powder and beat again until well combined. Do the same with the bananas.

Divide the mixture evenly between the muffin cases, filling each case to about two-thirds full. Bake in the centre of the oven for 25 minutes, until a skewer inserted into the centre of one of the cakes comes out clean. Leave the cupcakes to cool in their tin for 10 minutes and then turn out onto a wire rack.

When the cupcakes are completely cool, ice them with the caramel buttercream and decorate each cake with a couple of banana chips.

BREAKFAST

Breakfast is always a busy time for us, especially in our Primrose Hill shop where we are lucky to have lots of regular customers who live in the neighbourhood. Our croissants are much in demand and customers have been known to ring up to reserve them. They are all made by hand on a daily basis and, although croissants have a reputation as something that can only be made by a highly experienced pastry chef, in fact they are achievable by all. After sampling them on a recent trip to Italy, we now also make wholemeal and apricot jam-filled ones, which are proving popular.

Making your own great-tasting croissants is such a good feeling and not nearly as difficult as you might think! We've written our recipe, incorporating the strict technique all our bakers follow, so that novice bakers too can produce the same, much-loved, delicious croissants we serve fresh, straight from our ovens each morning. All you need is a little patience and strong bicep muscles.

CROISSANTS AND PAINS AU CHOCOLAT

300ml 'hand hot' water

1½ tsp active dried yeast

500g strong white bread flour, plus more for rolling

45g granulated sugar

2 tsp salt

20g skimmed milk powder

250g unsalted butter, preferably straight from the fridge

FOR THE PAINS AU CHOCOLAT

40g good-quality dark chocolate (at least 70% cocoa solids), broken into small pieces

FOR THE EGG WASH

2 large eggs, free-range or organic, beaten

Makes approx. 6 plain croissants and 4 pains au chocolat

Measure the water into a jug and stir in the yeast. Let it sit for 10 minutes until lightly foamy on top (this is how you can tell the yeast is active). Make sure the water isn't too hot or it will kill your yeast.

Sift all the dry ingredients into a large bowl and stir well with a wooden spoon. Cut the butter into small chunks and mix it through the dry ingredients, but do not overmix. Stir in the yeast mixture and combine until incorporated.

Wrap the dough in clingfilm and refrigerate overnight. You may find that the clingfilm blows up a bit as the gas comes out of the dough.

When you are ready to roll out your croissants amd pains au chocolat, flour a large, flat work surface and roll the dough into a large rectangle – don't worry too much at this stage about the depth. Fold the rectangle into thirds, as if folding a letter, and rotate the dough 90 degrees (see pictures overleaf). Repeat the rolling, folding and rotating process 3 more times.

After the fourth folding and rotating, roll the dough into a rectangle measuring 48 x 38cm. Follow the diagram on page 83 for instructions on cutting the croissants and pains au chocolat into shape. Then follow the pictures on page 84 for rolling them. Each pain au chocolat will need a small amount (about 10g) of dark chocolate, broken into small pieces.

Place the rolled croissants and pains au chocolat on a baking sheet lined with baking paper. If you don't want to cook these immediately, simply cover with clingfilm and return to the fridge, or freeze them for later.

 **BREAKFAST**

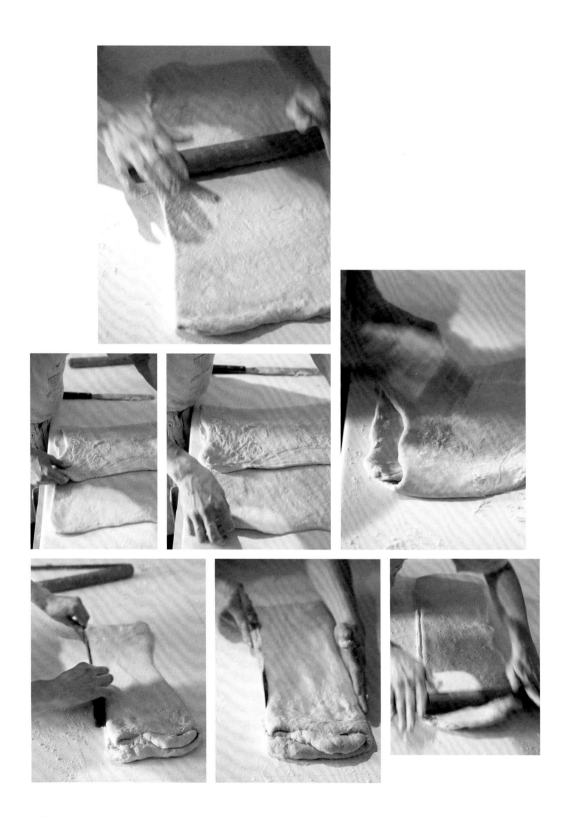

BREAKFAST

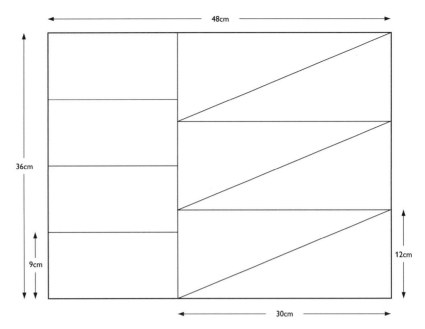

When you are ready to cook them, preheat the oven to 200°C/gas mark 6. Take the clingfilm off the croissants and pains au chocolat and leave them to sit at room temperature for at least 1 hour, during which time they will almost double in size.

Beat the eggs in a small cup or dish and brush each croissant and pain au chocolat with some of the beaten egg. Bake in the oven for about 30 minutes until golden brown and beginning to crisp up. These are delicious served immediately from the oven while still warm. They are best eaten on the day they are baked, but can be wrapped in clingfilm and refrigerated overnight ready for reheating the next day.

Jam filled Croissant

Add 1–1½ tablespoon apricot or peach jam to the centre of the dough before rolling into shape.

Wholemeal Croissant

Replace 250g of the strong white bread flour with strong wholemeal bread flour. Follow the same method.

 **BREAKFAST**

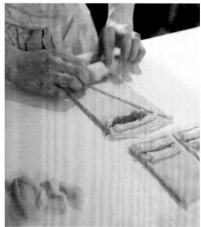

BREAKFAST

 BREAKFAST

These delicious spicy and sticky cinnamon buns are a new addition to our breakfast counters and this recipe was devised by one of our fantastic pastry chefs, Julia Murphy-Buske. Julia first made these in her native Canada on a cold day in Jasper, Alberta and now makes them for us to help us through the dreary English winters. For an even tastier result, you could spread them with our Cream Cheese Icing (see page 107).

CINNAMON BUNS

275g lukewarm water

5g active dried yeast

4 tbsp granulated sugar

600g strong white bread flour, sifted, plus more for rolling

¼ tsp salt

175g milk, warmed very slightly in a pan to 'hand hot'

75g unsalted butter, at room temperature

FOR THE FILLING

125g unsalted butter, at room temperature

250g dark brown sugar

1½ tsp ground cinnamon

½ tsp ground ginger

¼ tsp nutmeg

Pinch of cloves

FOR THE GLAZE

2 tbsp apricot jam mixed with 3 tbsp water

Makes 12 buns

Measure the water into a jug, then stir in the yeast and 1 tablespoon of the sugar and set aside.

Preheat the oven to 180°C/gas mark 4. Line a baking tray with baking paper.

In a large bowl mix together the flour, salt and the remaining 3 tablespoons sugar, using your hands or a spoon. Add the 75g butter and mix well. Add the milk and the yeast mixture and stir to form a sticky dough.

Turn the dough out onto a large, well-floured surface and, with well-floured hands, knead for about 5 minutes until smooth and elastic – the dough should spring back when touched. Allow the dough to rest.

After 10 minutes, roll the dough out to a rectangle measuring 63 x 38cm. Spread the 125g butter evenly over this rectangle, leaving a 2.5cm gap along the bottom (long) edge (see pictures overleaf). In a bowl mix together the brown sugar and all the spices and spread over the butter. Starting from the top of the rectangle, roll up the dough towards the bottom edge, enclosing the filling.

Brush the bottom edge with a little water to secure the dough you have just rolled and then cut the roll into 5cm lengths. Place on the baking tray and leave to rise for about 40 minutes in a warm area.

Bake in the oven for 18–20 minutes until golden brown. Remove from the oven and brush the apricot jam glaze over the hot buns. These are best served straight away, but any uneaten buns can be wrapped in clingfilm and refrigerated overnight and then reheated the next day.

  BREAKFAST

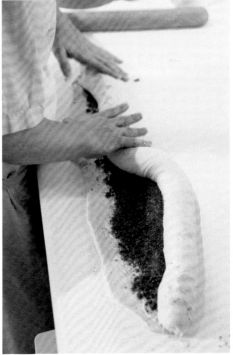

 **BREAKFAST**

Corn muffins are still relatively unknown as a breakfast treat in Britain. We were introduced to them by Martha's brother Daniel in New York, where he lives and where we eat them cut open, toasted and spread with grape jelly.

CORN MUFFINS

285g plain flour
230g yellow cornmeal or polenta flour
3 tbsp granulated sugar
2½ tsp baking powder
¼ tsp bicarbonate of soda
½ tsp salt
Pinch of nutmeg
230ml buttermilk (you can make your
 own by combining 230ml milk with
  2 tsp lemon juice)
3 tbsp unsalted butter, melted and cooled
3 tbsp corn oil
2 large eggs
3 tbsp honey

Makes 12 muffins

If you are making your own buttermilk, do this first and set aside.

Preheat the oven to 180°C/gas mark 4. Line a 12-hole muffin tray with muffin cases.

Sift the dry ingredients into a large bowl. Put the wet ingredients (buttermilk, butter, corn oil, eggs and honey) into a separate large bowl.

Add all the wet ingredients to the dry and, using an electric hand mixer, beat on a high setting for about 1 minute. Divide the mixture evenly between the muffin cases filling them two thirds full, and bake in the oven for 12–15 minutes until risen and golden brown.

You could serve these straight from the oven or allow to cool in the tin and then serve either cold or lightly toasted. Store any uneaten muffins in an airtight container for a couple of days.

 BREAKFAST

We started making our own granola when we opened our first shop in Primrose Hill and needed something quick and nutritious for our own breakfast. We always serve this with plain yoghurt and a seasonal fruit salad, but it's also good with just cold milk poured over. This is the granola we use in our Granola and White Chocolate Cookies on page 194.

GRANOLA

170g unsalted butter
250ml clear honey
2 tbsp golden syrup
500g rolled oats
250g whole almonds
250g sunflower seeds
200g pumpkin seeds
150g dried cranberries
150g dried blueberries
150g dried sour cherries
200g dried apricots

Makes enough to fill 1 x 1 litre jar

Preheat the oven to 180°C/gas mark 4. Line a baking tray with baking paper.

Melt the butter, honey and golden syrup in a heavy-based saucepan over a low heat until runny, stirring continuously.

Tip the oats, almonds, sunflower seeds and pumpkin seeds onto the lined baking tray and pour the warmed mixture over them. Bake in the oven until golden brown and a little bit crisp – this should take about 25 minutes. Be sure to rotate and stir the mix frequently while it is in the oven.

Once it is out of the oven, allow it to cool fully on the tray. Then add all the dried fruit and mix well with a spoon. Store in an airtight jar or other airtight container to maintain its freshness and crispness. Stored correctly, it should keep well for a few weeks.

This is our winter alternative to fruit salad – it's fantastic served on its own or with some hot porridge or granola. Our Scottish chef, Ryan, started making it for us recently when the winter weather became too cold to think about fresh fruit salad and the seasonal fruit was a little sparse and uninteresting. Once all the fruit has been stewed, the beautiful pinky orange colour will brighten your day before you even start eating this dish.

POACHED SPICED FRUIT

FOR THE SYRUP

1 litre water

500g golden caster sugar

1 cinnamon stick

2 star anise

6 whole cloves

**1 tsp good-quality vanilla extract
  or 1 vanilla pod**

Pinch of ground nutmeg

1 piece stem ginger, from a jar

FOR THE FRUIT

6 ripe pears

6 apples

6 plums

150g fresh cranberries

6 oranges

Makes approx. 8 servings

Put all the syrup ingredients into a large saucepan and bring to the boil on the hob. As soon as the syrup boils, turn off the heat and leave it to infuse while you prepare the fruit.

Peel and core the pears and apples and cut into small squares. Wash the plums and cut into quarters, removing the stones. Wash the cranberries. Peel the oranges and cut into segments (you can add any excess juice to the syrup).

Once the fruit is ready, bring the syrup back to the boil. Add the diced pears and simmer gently until just cooked but still a little firm – it is very important not to overcook them or they will begin to break up and become mushy. Remove the pears from the syrup with a slotted spoon and allow to cool on a plate.

Repeat this process for the apples and plums. Once these are done, add the cranberries to the syrup and simmer gently until cooked – these will require a bit more cooking than the other fruit, otherwise they will be a little sour. Once they are cooked, remove the pan from the heat and add the oranges. Allow everything to cool and then return the pears, apples and plums to the syrup.

Pour into a bowl and serve immediately (if you used a vanilla pod, you can spoon the fruit around it or remove it just before serving) or store in a covered jug or bowl in the fridge until needed. This is delicious served hot or cold and it will keep well for up to a week in the fridge.

 **BREAKFAST**

LAYER CAKES

Sometimes people think that Primrose Bakery is all about cupcakes – in fact, our layer cakes are equally popular and we bake and sell many birthday, wedding, christening (and even divorce) cakes. Whether they are personalised for a special occasion or simply left plain for afternoon tea, these cakes are always well received by our customers.

For the cakes in this chapter we have given quantities for making a 20cm (or in some cases 23cm) round cake, which will give you approximately 10 to 12 slices. Should you wish to make a larger, circular or even square cake, you can do this easily by increasing the quantities. As a general rule, cake tins should be filled to about two-thirds full with the mixture, to allow room for the cakes to rise, and the mixture should be evened out in the tin before baking.

There are occasions when nothing can beat the classic Victoria sponge. It's one of our bakery's all-time favourite cakes throughout the year and perhaps the most traditional English cake we do. This cake is best served as soon as it has cooled, been iced and placed on a beautiful vintage cake plate.

VICTORIA SPONGE

FOR THE SPONGE
210g self-raising flour
225g golden caster sugar
25g cornflour
1 tsp baking powder
1 tsp good-quality vanilla extract
225g unsalted butter, at room temperature and quite soft, plus more for greasing tins
4 large eggs, free-range or organic
3 tbsp semi-skimmed milk

FOR THE FILLING
2–3 tbsp good-quality strawberry or raspberry jam
½ batch Vanilla Buttercream Icing (see recipe on page 52) or 2 tbsp whipped double cream or whipping cream

FOR DECORATING
Icing sugar, for dusting
A few fresh strawberries or raspberries (optional)

Makes 2 x 20cm round cakes, which can be sandwiched together to make 1 layer cake

Preheat the oven to 180°C/gas mark 4. Grease 2 x 20cm sandwich cake tins and line the base of each tin with baking paper.

To make the sponge, sift the flour, sugar, cornflour and baking powder into a food processor and mix well. Add the remaining ingredients, and process briefly. Don't be tempted to leave the processor on and walk away as the batter will quickly overmix resulting in a heavier textured cake.

Divide the batter evenly between the 2 tins and smooth the tops with a spatula. Bake in the centre of the oven for about 25 minutes, until raised and golden brown and a skewer inserted into the centre of one of the cakes comes out clean. Leave the cakes to cool slightly in their tins for about 10 minutes before turning out onto wire racks.

Once the cakes are cool, remove the baking paper circles from their bases and lay 1 cake on a plate or cake stand. Spread with a thin layer of raspberry or strawberry jam. Then, holding the other cake in your hand, spread its underside with 2 or 3 good spoonfuls of the vanilla buttercream icing or freshly whipped cream. Sandwich the 2 layers together and sprinkle the top with icing sugar. You could also add a layer of finely sliced strawberries or raspberries in the middle if you wanted.

Any leftover cake will keep well for a couple of days in an airtight tin at room temperature. If you have used fresh cream and fruit, store in the fridge overnight.

 LAYER CAKES

A pretty pink cake with strawberries in the sponge, in the filling and on the top, this is the perfect summer treat.

STRAWBERRY CAKE

FOR THE SPONGE

210g self-raising flour

25g cornflour

225g golden caster sugar

1 tsp baking powder

**225g unsalted butter, at room temp-
erature, plus more for greasing tins**

4 large eggs, free-range or organic

**225g fresh strawberries, hulled and
chopped into small pieces**

1 tsp good-quality vanilla extract

**250g fresh strawberries, hulled,
to decorate**

FOR THE FILLING

3–4 tbsp strawberry jam

**1 batch Vanilla Buttercream Icing
(see recipe on page 52), coloured
pale pink with a few drops of rose
food colouring**

**A few fresh strawberries, hulled
and sliced**

Makes 2 x 20cm round cakes, which can be sandwiched together to make 1 layer cake

Preheat the oven to 180°C/gas mark 4. Grease 2 x 20cm sandwich cake tins and line the base of each tin with baking paper.

Sift the flour, cornflour, sugar and baking powder into the bowl of a food processor. Pulse until evenly mixed, which should take about 4 seconds. Add the butter, eggs, strawberries and vanilla extract and process briefly until well combined, but not overly processed.

Divide the mixture evenly between the 2 cake tins and smooth the tops with a spatula. Bake in the centre of the oven for 25 minutes, until a skewer inserted into the centre of one of the cakes comes out clean.

Leave the cakes to cool slightly in their tins for 10 minutes and then turn out onto wire racks.

When the cakes are completely cool, remove the baking paper circles from their bases. Place 1 cake on a plate and spread with a thin layer of strawberry jam. Then place a thin layer of sliced strawberries on top of the jam. Hold the second cake and ice the under-side of it with a 1cm-thick layer of vanilla buttercream. Carefully place on top of the first cake, iced side down. Once the cakes are sandwiched together, ice the top with the remaining buttercream and top with the fresh strawberries.

This cake is best served immediately, as the fresh strawberries do have a tendency to soften and bleed their juice into the icing quite quickly.

  LAYER CAKES

 **LAYER CAKES**

Carrot cake is often perceived to be healthier and less sweet than many other cakes and is usually enjoyed by all. The moist, fruity sponge works brilliantly with the smooth, cool cream cheese icing for a tasty treat at any time of day.

CARROT CAKE

FOR THE SPONGE

450g grated carrots

260g raisins

4 large eggs, free-range or organic

260g golden caster sugar

240ml corn oil

1 tsp good-quality vanilla extract

4 tsp fresh orange zest

240g plain flour

2 tsp bicarbonate of soda

Pinch of salt

2 tsp cinnamon, plus more for dusting

Butter, for greasing tins

FOR THE FILLING AND TOPPING

1 batch Cream Cheese Icing
 (see recipe overleaf)

Makes 2 x 20cm round cakes, which can be sandwiched together to form 1 layer cake, plus 6 regular carrot cupcakes

Preheat the oven to 180°C/gas mark 4. Grease 2 x 20cm sandwich cake tins and line the base of each tin with baking paper. Line a 12-hole muffin tray with 6 muffin cases.

Combine the grated carrots and raisins in a large bowl, and put to one side. In another bowl beat the eggs and sugar together with an electric hand mixer for several minutes and then carefully add the oil, vanilla extract and orange zest and beat well.

Sift the flour, bicarbonate of soda, salt and cinnamon into a separate bowl and then slowly add these ingredients to the egg and sugar mixture, beating well after each addition. Pour this mixture into the bowl containing the carrots and raisins and mix with a wooden spoon or spatula until well incorporated.

Fill each cake tin to about two-thirds full and then divide any remaining mixture between the muffin cases in the muffin tray. Bake for about 30 minutes, until golden brown and a spatula inserted into the centre of one of the cakes comes out clean. Allow the cakes to cool in their tins for 10 minutes or so before turning out onto wire racks to cool completely.

When you are ready to assemble the cake, remove the baking paper from the bases. Place 1 cake on a plate and spread with a generous amount of icing. Carefully place the other cake on top and ice the top with more icing. Sprinkle with a dusting of cinnamon.

If you have made some cupcakes too, you can ice them the same way.

 LAYER CAKES

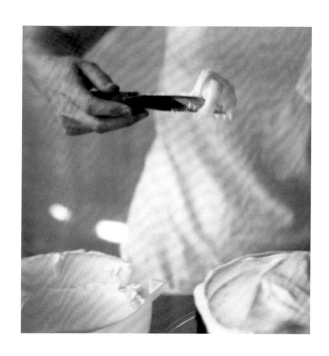

CREAM CHEESE ICING

175g cream cheese, at room temperature
450g icing sugar, sifted
125g unsalted butter, at room temperature
Zest from 1 orange

Makes enough to ice 1 x 20cm round layer cake with some left over

Place all the ingredients in a mixing bowl and beat well with an electric hand mixer until they are thoroughly combined and the icing is smooth and pale.

As this icing contains cream cheese, it must be stored in the fridge, where it will keep well for 3–4 days. Before reusing, let it come to room temperature and then beat again.

 LAYER CAKES

The pale pink colour of this finished cake fits in perfectly with the colours of our shops and our other cakes and looks even better if sitting on a green plate, as the colours work so well together. It feels like a very summery cake, but really could be eaten at any time of the year and you could always substitute the desiccated coconut on top with some toasted coconut flakes or even some marshmallows.

COCONUT CAKE

FOR THE SPONGE

170g desiccated coconut

150ml water

250g unsalted butter, plus more for greasing tin

330g golden caster sugar

1 tsp good-quality vanilla extract

4 large egg whites

375g self-raising flour, sifted

FOR THE FILLING AND TOPPING

1 batch Vanilla Buttercream Icing (see recipe on page 52), coloured with a few drops of pink food colouring

Desiccated coconut, to decorate

Makes 1 x 23cm round cake

Preheat the oven to 180°C/gas mark 4. Grease 1 x 23cm cake tin (about 6–7cm in depth) and line the base with baking paper.

Put the coconut and water in a bowl and stir to combine. Leave to one side.

Using an electric hand mixer or a freestanding mixer, beat the butter, sugar and vanilla extract for 8–10 minutes until pale and creamy. Gradually add the egg whites, beating well after each addition. Add the coconut mixture and the flour and beat well to combine.

Pour the mixture into the cake tin and smooth the top with a spatula. Bake in the centre of the oven for about 1½ hours, until the top is golden brown in colour and a skewer inserted into the centre of the cake comes out clean. With so much coconut in it, the sponge will be fairly moist.

Leave the cake to cool in its tin for about 10 minutes before turning it out onto a wire rack.

When the cake is completely cool, remove the baking paper, then spread the pink buttercream icing all over the top and sides and sprinkle with the coconut. Do this quite quickly before the icing sets too much or the coconut won't stick on.

Any uneaten cake can be kept for 2–3 days in an airtight container or wrapped in clingfilm and stored at room temperature.

  LAYER CAKES

Easily adapted from our chocolate cupcake recipe, this 3-tiered, caramel-drenched cake should satisfy even your diehard Dime bar-loving guest. As the consistency of the icing is runnier than most of our others, let it cascade over each layer for a mouth-watering finish.

TRIPLE LAYER CARAMEL CAKE

FOR THE SPONGE

2 batches chocolate sponge batter (see recipe for Cookies and Cream Cupcakes on page 21)

FOR THE ICING

1 batch Caramel Buttercream Icing (see overleaf)
Butter, for greasing tin

Makes 3 x 20cm round cakes, which can be sandwiched together to make 1 layer cake

Preheat the oven to 190°C/gas mark 5. Grease 3 x 20cm sandwich cake tins and line the bases with baking paper.

Divide the batter evenly between the tins (use between 500g and 600g batter in each tin) and smooth the tops with a spatula. Bake in the centre of the oven for about 30 minutes, until a skewer inserted into the centre of one of the cakes comes out clean. Leave the cakes to cool slightly in their tins for about 10 minutes before turning them out onto wire racks to cool completely.

Remove the sheets of baking paper from the bases of the cakes. Ice the top of each cake with the caramel buttercream and allow it to set a little before sandwiching the cakes together and serving.

Un-iced, these sponge layers can be wrapped in clingfilm and kept at room temperature for up to 3 days, or even frozen and then defrosted when needed.

 LAYER CAKES

CARAMEL BUTTERCREAM ICING

90g unsalted butter
135ml (9 tbsp) semi-skimmed milk
330g light, soft brown sugar
360g icing sugar, sifted
1 tsp good-quality vanilla extract

Makes enough to ice 1 x 20cm triple layer cake

Combine the butter, milk and brown sugar in a heavy-based saucepan and put on the hob over a high heat. Stirring continuously, bring the mixture to a boil. Allow it to boil for 1 minute, then remove from the heat and stir in half of the icing sugar.

Allow the mixture to cool slightly, then add the rest of the icing sugar and the vanilla extract and stir until it thickens to the desired consistency. It will have a slightly runny consistency, which works well with this cake. If you leave it and it starts to set, just transfer to a microsafe bowl and soften it for a few seconds in the microwave before beating again and, if necessary, add a little double cream.

Store any unused icing in the fridge, where it should keep well for up to a week. If using straight from the fridge, you will need to let it come to room temperature and beat well.

 **LAYER CAKES**

  **LAYER CAKES**

We are often asked for gluten-free cupcakes, but have not yet had time to develop them. Instead, a friend of Lisa's, an amazing organic skincare specialist called Sharon McGlinchey, sent us this recipe and we often eat it all before it reaches the shop counter!

FLOURLESS CHOCOLATE CAKE

200g good-quality dark chocolate (at least 70% cocoa solids), broken into small pieces

200g unsalted butter, plus more for greasing tin

4 large eggs, free-range or organic, separated

220g golden caster sugar

Cocoa powder or icing sugar, sifted, for dusting (optional)

Makes 1 x 23cm round cake

Preheat the oven to 180°C/gas mark 4. Grease and line 1 x 23cm cake tin (preferably one with a removable base).

Melt the chocolate pieces and the butter in a heatproof bowl set over a saucepan of simmering water, stirring continually. In another large bowl, beat the egg yolks with half of the caster sugar, using an electric hand mixer. Fold in the melted chocolate and butter until well combined.

In a separate, clean bowl and using a whisk or an electric hand mixer, whisk the egg whites to soft peaks and then beat in the remaining sugar. Fold this mixture into the first bowl with the other sponge ingredients, being careful not to overmix otherwise you will knock too much air out of the mixture. Pour the batter into the prepared tin and bake in the centre of the oven for about 40 minutes, or until a skewer inserted into the centre of the cake comes out clean.

Leave the cake to cool in its tin for about 10 minutes before turning out onto a wire rack to cool completely.

This cake will have a fairly sticky, fudge-like consistency and would be delicious served warm or cold, on its own or with some cream or ice-cream. You could dust the top with some cocoa or icing sugar before serving if desired. Any uneaten cake will keep very well for a good few days either in an airtight container or wrapped in clingfilm and stored at room temperature.

 LAYER CAKES

This is the favourite cake of Lisa's nephew, Gareth, who works in our bakeries. His coffee-making skills are renowned, and one of his cappuccinos would go perfectly with a slice of this (or, indeed, any other cake – as he would be the first to tell you!)

ORANGE CAKE

FOR THE SPONGE

225g unsalted butter, at room temperature, plus more for greasing tin
225g golden caster sugar
Zest of 1 small orange
4 large eggs, free-range or organic
225g self-raising flour, sifted

FOR THE ORANGE BUTTERCREAM

125g unsalted butter
15ml freshly squeezed orange juice
150g icing sugar, sifted
Zest of ½ small orange

FOR THE GLAZE

200g icing sugar, sifted
2 tbsp freshly squeezed orange juice

Makes 2 x 20cm round cakes, which can be sandwiched together to make 1 layer cake

Preheat the oven to 180°C/gas mark 4. Grease 2 x 20cm sandwich cake tins and line the base of each tin with baking paper.

To make the sponge, cream the butter, sugar and orange zest in a large bowl with an electric hand mixer. Add the eggs, one at a time, beating well after each addition. If the mixture curdles a little, add some of the flour. Gradually add the remaining flour and beat well, but not for too long.

Divide the mixture evenly between the 2 tins and smooth the tops with a spatula. Bake in the centre of the oven for 20–25 minutes, until raised and golden brown and a skewer inserted into the centre of one of the cakes comes out clean. Allow the cakes to cool in their tins for 10 minutes before turning out onto wire racks to cool completely.

To make the orange buttercream, beat the butter, orange juice and half the icing sugar together in a bowl. Gradually add the remainder of the icing sugar and then the orange zest and beat until smooth.

To make the glaze, gently pour the orange juice into a bowl containing the icing sugar and beat on a low speed with an electric hand mixer. The glaze should be of a slightly runny, liquid consistency.

To assemble the layer cake, spread the top of 1 cake with the orange buttercream and place the other on top. Pour the glaze carefully and evenly over the top of the cake, allowing some of it to run over the sides. Decorate with orange zest. Allow the glaze to set a little before serving. Best eaten on the day of baking.

 **LAYER CAKES**

 LAYER CAKES

When we first started supplying cakes to the delicatessen Melrose and Morgan in 2004, this is one of the cakes we made quite often. It comes from a 1980s American recipe book by Jim Fobel, which was given to us by Martha's brother, Daniel. Its spicy, nutty, fruit flavour makes a delicious alternative to some of the sweeter cakes.

APPLE CAKE

300g plain flour
2 tsp bicarbonate of soda
1 tsp baking powder
1½ tsp ground cinnamon
1 tsp freshly grated nutmeg
¼ tsp ground cloves
170g raisins
115g chopped walnuts
120g unsalted butter, at room temperature, plus more for greasing tin
230g granulated sugar
1 large egg, free-range or organic
2 tsp good-quality vanilla extract
500g apple sauce (from a jar) or unsweetened stewed apple
Icing sugar, for dusting

Makes 1 x 23cm round cake

Preheat the oven to 180°C/gas mark 4. Grease 1 x 23cm cake tin (about 6–7cm in depth) and line the base with baking paper.

Sift the flour, bicarbonate of soda and baking powder into a medium-sized bowl, add the cinnamon, nutmeg and cloves and mix well with a wooden spoon. In a separate bowl, combine the raisins and walnuts and then add a small amount of the flour mixture to coat them well.

In another bowl, cream the butter and sugar for a minute or two with an electric hand mixer, until the mixture is light and fluffy. Add the egg and the vanilla extract and beat well. Beat in the flour mixture, one-third at a time, alternating with the apple sauce. Finally, stir in the walnut and raisin mixture with a spoon until well combined.

Pour the mixture into the prepared cake tin, making sure the batter is evenly distributed. Bake in the centre of the oven for about 40 minutes, until the top is golden brown and a skewer inserted into the centre of the cake comes out clean. Let it cool in its tin on a wire rack before turning out onto a serving plate.

Dust a little icing sugar over the top of the cake before serving. You could also serve it still slightly warm and even with double cream or crème fraiche.

Keep any uneaten cake in an airtight container or wrap in clingfilm and store at room temperature for 2–3 days.

This moist, spicy banana cake can be made and served with or without a sour cream chocolate icing, depending on the occasion. A slice without icing would make a delicious breakfast, while the addition of the bittersweet icing turns it into a rich afternoon treat. Our former chef Frances – who sadly has moved back to the US – first made it for Martha's daughter Daisy, who wanted to try a banana cake without chocolate chips (having been brought up on our Chocolate and Banana Loaf, page 147).

BANANA CAKE

400g plain flour

2 tsp baking soda

280g unsalted butter, at room temperature, plus more for greasing tin

200ml (90g) sour cream

3 tsp good-quality vanilla extract

4 tsp grated lemon zest

350g golden caster sugar

4 large eggs, free-range or organic

500g mashed banana (the riper and softer the bananas the better)

1 batch Sour Cream Chocolate Icing (optional, see recipe opposite)

Makes 1 x 23cm round cake

Preheat the oven to 180°C/gas mark 4. Grease and line a 23cm cake tin (about 6–7cm in depth).

Sift the flour and baking soda into a large bowl and stir together. Add the butter and beat well with an electric hand mixer, until the mixture is pale and creamy.

In a separate bowl, mix the sour cream, vanilla extract and lemon zest together and then beat into the flour mixture. Gradually add the sugar and then the eggs, one at a time, beating well after each addition. Add the mashed banana and mix until everything is combined.

Pour the batter into the prepared cake tin, making sure it is evenly distributed throughout the tin. Bake in the centre of the oven for 2 hours, until a skewer inserted into the centre of the cake comes out clean. Allow the cake to cool in its tin for about 10 minutes and then turn out onto a wire rack to cool completely.

The cake can be served without icing, and even while slightly warm. Alternatively, once the cake has cooled completely, spread the Sour Cream Chocolate Icing over the top and the sides in a thin layer and allow it to set a little before serving.

Any uneaten, un-iced cake can be kept for 2–3 days in an airtight container or wrapped in clingfilm and stored at room temperature.

SOUR CREAM CHOCOLATE ICING

**350g good-quality dark chocolate
(at least 70% cocoa solids), broken
into pieces**
400ml (360g) sour cream

Makes enough to ice 1 x 23cm round cake

Melt the chocolate together with the sour cream, either in a microsafe bowl in the microwave or in a pan over a low heat, beating continually. Once the chocolate is melted you should have a smooth icing, which you can then use to cover the top and sides of the banana cake. Allow it to set a little before serving.

 LAYER CAKES

This is definitely a winter cake and it's perfect served with fresh cream or crème fraîche. Our staff and customers are always excited when it reappears on our shop counters after its long summer holiday and it's a particular favourite of one of our longest-serving members of staff, Emma, who always takes a slice of it home after a long day at work to enjoy it slowly rather than rushing to eat it in between serving customers.

PEAR AND GINGER CAKE

FOR THE SPONGE

230g plain flour, sifted
½ tsp bicarbonate of soda
½ tsp salt
115g soft brown sugar
½ tsp ground nutmeg
½ tsp ground cloves
1 tbsp ground cinnamon
½ tbsp ground ginger
1½ pieces stem ginger, chopped
  into small pieces (reserve the juice)
1 tbsp ginger juice, from above
  stem ginger
2 large eggs, free-range or organic,
  beaten
120ml buttermilk
65g unsalted butter, melted, plus
  more for greasing tin

FOR THE TOPPING

60g unsalted butter, softened
115g soft brown sugar
2–3 ripe pears, peeled and sliced

Makes 1 x 20cm round cake

Preheat the oven to 180°C/gas mark 4. Grease a 20cm sandwich cake tin (about 4–5cm in depth), very well. Ideally, use a springform tin so it's easier to get the cake out later.

Make the topping first, by creaming the butter and sugar together in a bowl, using an electric hand mixer, until the mixture is pale and fluffy. Spoon this into the base of the prepared cake tin, spreading it evenly and smoothing the top with a spatula. Arrange the pear slices over the top, placing them in a fan-like pattern around the edge of the tin.

To make the sponge, sift the flour, bicarbonate of soda, salt, brown sugar and the ground spices into a large bowl, add the pieces of stem ginger and the ginger juice and mix with an electric hand mixer or a wooden spoon until well combined. Gradually add the beaten eggs, buttermilk and melted butter and beat on a low speed to make a smooth batter. Pour this batter into the tin over the pears, making sure it is evenly distributed.

Bake in the centre of the oven for about 1 hour, until golden brown and a skewer inserted into the centre of the cake comes out clean. Leave the cake to cool in its tin for about 10 minutes and then very carefully invert it onto a wire rack, so that the pears will be visible at the top of the cake.

This cake can be served warm or cold and is best eaten on the same day or the day after baking for optimum freshness.

 LAYER CAKES

Our popular plum cake came to us via one of our favourite Australian chefs, Bill Granger. His books are full of interesting and simple recipes that seem to epitomise the sunny, sociable, outdoors lifestyle in Australia. We serve this cake almost every day in our shops and if it's not there, customers always ask for it. You could even serve it with cream or ice-cream as a dessert after dinner.

PLUM CAKE

FOR THE SPONGE
185g plain flour
2 tsp baking powder
180g unsalted butter, at room
  temperature, plus more
  for greasing
250g golden caster sugar
1 tsp good-quality vanilla extract
3 large eggs, free-range or organic,
  lightly beaten
500g good-quality ripe plums,
  stoned and quartered

FOR THE TOPPING
90g soft dark brown sugar
90g plain flour
100g unsalted butter, at room
  temperature

Makes 1 x 25cm round cake

Preheat the oven to 180°C/gas mark 4. Grease and line a 25cm cake tin (about 6–7cm in depth).

Sift the flour and baking powder together into a large bowl and mix well.

In another large bowl cream the butter and caster sugar with an electric hand mixer until the mixture is pale and fluffy. Add the vanilla extract and mix well, then gradually add the beaten eggs and beat until just combined. Slowly add the flour and baking powder and beat well on a low speed.

Pour the batter into the prepared tin and smooth it over with a spatula so that it is evenly distributed. Arrange a circle of plum quarters on top, around the edge of the tin and then fill in the centre with the remainder of the plums.

To make the topping, sift the flour and brown sugar into a bowl, add the butter and mix with your hands or with an electric hand mixer until large crumbs are formed and the mixture starts to come together. Sprinkle over the top of the plums, covering them completely.

Bake in the centre of the oven for about 1–1¼ hours (do not open the door while it is cooking). When the cake is cooked, a skewer inserted into the centre should come out clean. Allow it to cool in its tin for at least 15 minutes before turning out onto a wire rack.

This cake is delicious served slightly warm, although it will keep well for 2–3 days in an airtight container at room temperature.

Ginger, spice and cream — and not a soaked raisin or sultana in sight — this is the Victoria sponge for the Christmas season, with its light cinnamon, ginger and clove sponge sandwiched together with ginger whipped cream. It makes the perfect afternoon treat with a cup of tea or a glass of mulled wine.

GINGER CREAM CHRISTMAS CAKE

FOR THE SPONGE
2 tbsp finely chopped fresh ginger
1 tbsp golden caster sugar
250g self-raising flour
2 tsp ground ginger
¾ tsp ground cinnamon
¼ tsp ground cloves
165g unsalted butter, at room temperature, plus more for greasing tins
175g soft light brown sugar
3 large eggs, free-range or organic
125ml golden syrup
185g good-quality dark chocolate (at least 70% cocoa solids)
250ml buttermilk
Icing sugar, for dusting

FOR THE FILLING
250ml double or whipping cream
8 slices peeled fresh ginger

Makes 2 x 20cm round cakes, which can be sandwiched together to make 1 layer cake

Prepare the filling in advance. Place the cream and ginger in a saucepan over a medium heat and bring almost to boiling point. Remove from the heat and transfer to a bowl, then cover and place in the fridge for at least 2 hours, or ideally overnight. Before using strain the cream into a bowl, then whip.

To make the cake, preheat the oven to 180°C/gas mark 4. Grease 2 x 20cm cake tins and line the bases with baking paper. Put the fresh ginger and caster sugar in a bowl, stir and set aside for a few minutes. Sift the flour and spices together into a separate bowl and mix.

Melt 60g of the chocolate either in a heatproof bowl set over a pan of simmering water, or carefully in a microsafe bowl in the microwave. Leave to cool. Finely chop the remainder of the chocolate.

In a separate bowl, cream the butter and brown sugar together until pale and fluffy. Beat in the eggs, one by one. Don't worry if the mixture looks a little curdled. Beat in the golden syrup until smooth. Beat in the melted chocolate and the sugared ginger. Gradually add alternate spoonfuls of the spiced flour and the buttermilk, beating until the ingredients are just blended. Finally, fold in the chocolate.

Divide the mixture evenly between the tins. Bake in the centre of the oven for about 30 minutes, until a skewer inserted into the centre of one of the cakes comes out clean. Allow to cool in their tins for 10 minutes and then turn out onto wire racks.

Once completely cool, cover one cake generously with the cream, then place the other cake on top and spread with a further layer. This is best eaten on the day it is made, but can be stored overnight in the fridge.

 **LAYER CAKES**

  **LAYER CAKES**

The recipe for this delicious fruit cake comes from Lisa's mother, Marlene, in Australia. We never used to make fruit cake but this one tastes so good, we simply had to start doing it. Combining it with the brandy buttercream icing makes a luxurious (and more delicious, in our opinion) alternative to the traditional fondant icing.

MARLENE'S CHRISTMAS CAKE WITH BRANDY BUTTERCREAM ICING

175g sultanas
175g pitted dates, halved
175g currants
175g raisins
45g mixed peel
250ml ginger ale
50ml brandy
225g unsalted butter, at room temperature, plus more for greasing tin
200g golden caster sugar
4 large eggs, free-range or organic
250g plain flour
1 tsp baking powder
¼ tsp grated lemon zest
½ tsp good-quality vanilla extract
½ tsp almond extract

FOR THE TOPPING
1 batch Brandy Buttercream Icing (see recipe on page 47)
Festive cake decorations of your choice (optional)

Makes 1 x 20cm round cake

The day before you want to make the cake, combine the sultanas, dates, currants, raisins and peel with the ginger ale and brandy in a large bowl. Cover and leave to sit in a warm place overnight.

The next day, preheat oven to 180°C/gas mark 4. Grease 1 x 20cm cake tin (about 9cm in depth), and line the base with baking paper.

Using an electric hand mixer, cream the butter and sugar in a bowl until the mixture is pale and fluffy. Add the eggs, one by one, beating well after each addition.

Sift the flour and baking powder together into another bowl and then stir into the creamed mixture, using a wooden spoon. Drain the dried fruit and discard any excess liquid. Add this fruit, together with the lemon zest and vanilla and almond extracts, to the mixture and mix well.

Spoon the mixture into the prepared tin and smooth the top with a spatula. Bake in the centre of the oven for about 1 hour and 25 minutes, until a skewer inserted into the centre of the cake comes out clean. Allow the cake to cool completely in its tin before turning out onto a cake board or serving plate.

Spread the brandy buttercream all over the top and the sides of the cake, creating a snow-like effect, and decorate as desired with festive cake decorations of your choice.

This cake will keep well for 2–3 weeks in an airtight container or wrapped in clingfilm and stored at room temperature.

Icebox cake is one of the greatest American desserts of all time and very simple to prepare. We first experienced it on a hotter than hot Manhattan afternoon and it was unforgettable. It is traditionally made with Nabisco wafers, but as these are not easily available in the UK, we experimented with our own Bourbon Biscuits and added different flavours to the cream. They all worked out to make an equally delicious version of its original form. A succession of hot afternoons to eat it on would be great!

PRIMROSE BAKERY ICEBOX CAKE

900ml double or whipping cream
3 tbsp granulated sugar
1 tbsp good-quality vanilla extract
1 batch (40 circles) Aunt Mary's Bourbon Biscuits (see recipe on page 177)
1 small bar good-quality dark chocolate (at least 70% cocoa solids), grated, to decorate (optional)

Makes 1 x 20cm round cake

Put the cream, sugar and vanilla extract in a bowl and beat with an electric hand mixer until the cream is lightly whipped. Be very careful not to over-beat or it will ruin the finished cake.

Lay 12 of the bourbon circles on a flat, round plate to create a mostly filled-in, larger circle. Using about a quarter of the cream, spread it evenly across the biscuit base. Put another layer of 12 biscuits on top of the cream and spread with another quarter of the cream on top of this. Repeat this process until all the biscuits and cream are used up, finishing with a layer of cream. You could then grate some dark chocolate over the top, to finish.

Put the cake in the fridge for at least 5 hours (or overnight) to set. Serve straight from the fridge and cut as you would a sponge layer cake. Once set, it's best eaten straight away, but any uneaten cake can be stored in the fridge overnight.

As an alternative, you could make a chocolate-orange version by adding some orange zest to the cream and grating a Terry's Chocolate Orange over the top.

This is a new addition to our birthday cake range and you can use any flavour sponge, not just the one we recommend here. It is always good to use a different colour around the base or 'case' part of the sponge and the top 'icing' part of the sponge to differentiate between them but this is not essential. You will need a giant cupcake tin.

GIANT CUPCAKE

1 batch Victoria sponge (see recipe for Victoria Sponge on page 98)
1–2 batches Vanilla Buttercream Icing (see recipe on page 52)
Food colourings of your choice
Edible sprinkles or other cake decorations of your choice
Butter, for greasing tin

Makes 1 giant cupcake, approx. 16cm in diameter, which can be cut into 10–15 slices

Preheat the oven to 180°C/gas mark 4. Grease 1 giant cupcake tin well – if the sponge sticks it could break apart and lose its distinctive shape.

Make up the Victoria sponge as per the recipe and spoon about two-thirds of the batter into the base of the tin and spoon the remaining batter in the top of the tin.

Bake in the centre of the oven for 40–45 minutes, until golden brown and a skewer inserted into one of the cakes comes out clean. Allow to cool in the tin for about 10 minutes and then very carefully turn the 2 sponges out onto wire racks to finish cooling.

Make up the vanilla buttercream and divide it between 2 bowls. Add enough food colouring to each bowl to achieve your desired shades.

To ice the cake, place the base of the sponge on a silver cake board and level off the top with a knife so that the other sponge will sit on top and stay put. Spread one of the bowls of buttercream all over the base – you could even make the shape of a paper case in icing by using a knife to make thin stripes up the sides in the ridges of the cake.

Place the top part of the cake on the base and push down gently so that it sticks on. Spread the second bowl of buttercream icing around the top of the cake, and decorate as you wish.

This is quite a fragile cake and could topple over, so it's not a good idea to travel too far with it. Any uneaten cake can be stored in an airtight container at room temperature for 3–4 days.

LOAVES AND SLICES

We are always surprised at how popular a simple loaf cake can be in our shops, where we usually sell them by the slice and vary the flavours according to the time of year. Perhaps it's because they are, on the whole, a little less sweet than some of our cupcakes and layer cakes and make a nice alternative to have with a cup of coffee or tea, when a whole iced cupcake can seem too much.

Likewise our slices, which owe a lot to Lisa's New Zealand and Australian upbringing. We tend not to make these on a daily basis, but whenever we do, they get snapped up. Our friands, which are similar to French 'financier' cakes, are much loved in the tea room at Miller Harris in Mayfair, London.

We employ four Mongolian chefs in our kitchens, whose lack of spoken English is more than made up for by their very accurate and efficient baking. This lemon drizzle loaf is one of our favourite loaves and has been developed to perfection by one of the Mongolians, Baggi, who slightly altered the amount of lemon juice from our original recipe and produced an even better result.

LEMON DRIZZLE LOAF CAKE

FOR THE LOAF

155g self-raising flour, sifted
1 tsp baking powder
155g golden caster sugar
20g cornflour
155g unsalted butter, at room temperature, plus more for greasing tin
3 large eggs, free-range or organic
Grated zest and juice of 1 lemon

FOR THE DRIZZLE

160g granulated sugar
Juice of 2 lemons

Makes 1 x 900g loaf cake (8–10 slices)

Preheat the oven to 180°C/gas mark 4. Grease 1 x 900g loaf tin and line with baking paper or a loaf tin liner.

Sift the flour, baking powder, sugar and cornflour into the bowl of a food processor. Pulse the mixture for about 4 seconds until evenly mixed. Add the butter, eggs and lemon zest and juice and process briefly until evenly blended (about 10 seconds).

Pour the mixture into the loaf tin and level the top with a spatula. Bake in the centre of the oven for about 35–40 minutes, until golden brown and a skewer inserted into the centre of the loaf comes out clean. Let the loaf cool in its tin.

Make up the drizzle by stirring the sugar into the lemon juice in a jug and mixing well. Prick the surface of the loaf all over with a fork. Pour the drizzle over the loaf and allow it to set, before removing the loaf from the tin and serving. Keep any uneaten loaf in an airtight container at room temperature for 3–4 days.

This quite unassuming loaf cake, with its sweet blueberries and tart apples, has steadily grown in popularity and rightly earned its place as a regular on our bakeries' countertops. The still-warm slices are often chosen by our early morning customers to accompany the first coffee of the day.

APPLE AND BLUEBERRY LOAF

125g cold unsalted butter, cubed,
  plus more for greasing tin
225g self-raising flour, sifted
Pinch of salt
175g golden caster sugar
2 large eggs, free-range or organic,
  lightly beaten
2 apples (Granny Smiths work well),
  peeled, cored and thinly sliced
125g fresh blueberries
2 tbsp apricot jam

Makes 1 x 900g loaf cake (8–10 slices)

Preheat the oven to 190°C/gas mark 5. Grease 1 x 900g loaf tin and line with baking paper or a loaf tin liner.

Sift the flour, salt and butter into the bowl of a food processor and process until it has the texture of breadcrumbs. Add the sugar and eggs and mix again until smooth.

Carefully spoon the batter into the loaf tin and then scatter with half the apples and half the blueberries. Add the remaining batter and then arrange the remaining fruit over the top. Bake in the centre of the oven for about 1 hour until risen and quite firm to the touch. When the cake is cooked, a skewer inserted into the centre should come out clean.

Meanwhile, heat the apricot jam in a small pan over a low heat or in a microsafe dish in the microwave, to soften it. As soon as the loaf is out of the oven, brush the warm jam over it with a pastry brush. Allow to cool slightly in the tin for about 10 minutes before transferring to a wire rack. It's delicious eaten warm or cold.

Keep any uneaten loaf in an airtight container or wrapped in clingfilm for a couple of days or so.

 **LOAVES AND SLICES**

This spicy moist loaf cake makes the perfect breakfast or teatime treat – try eating it toasted and spread with butter.

GINGER LOAF

200g unsalted butter, diced, plus more for greasing tin
175g molasses sugar
3 tbsp black treacle/molasses
150ml semi-skimmed milk
4 pieces stem ginger, drained and chopped (reserve the syrup to pour over finished loaf)
2 large eggs, free-range or organic, beaten
300g self-raising flour
1 tbsp ground ginger
Pinch of salt

Makes 1 x 900g loaf cake (8–10 slices)

Preheat the oven to 180°C/gas mark 4. Grease 1 x 900g loaf tin and line with baking paper or a loaf tin liner.

Melt the butter, sugar and treacle in a saucepan over a low heat. Leave to cool briefly and then stir in the milk. In a bowl, add the chopped ginger to the beaten eggs and then beat into the butter mixture. Sift the flour, ground ginger and salt into a bowl, then add to the warm mixture and combine thoroughly.

Pour the mixture into the loaf tin and level it out with a spatula. Bake in the centre of the oven for 50 minutes, until a skewer inserted into the centre of the cake comes out clean.

Leave in the tin to cool. While it is cooling, prick the surface of the loaf all over with a fork, then pour the reserved ginger syrup over the loaf and brush it evenly all over.

Any uneaten ginger loaf can be kept in an airtight container or wrapped in clingfilm and stored at room temperature for 3–4 days.

The combination of banana and chocolate in this loaf cake is hard to resist. A slice of it served almost straight from the oven would be good for a winter breakfast or an afternoon tea.

CHOCOLATE AND BANANA LOAF

125g unsalted butter, at room temperature, plus more for greasing tin

250g golden caster sugar

2 large eggs, free-range or organic, lightly beaten

1 tsp good-quality vanilla extract

250g plain flour

2 tsp baking powder

4 ripe bananas, mashed with a fork

175g good-quality dark chocolate chips or dark chocolate (70% cocoa solids), broken into small pieces

Makes 1 x 900g loaf cake (8–10 slices)

Preheat the oven to 180°C/gas mark 4. Grease 1 x 900g loaf tin and line with baking paper or a loaf tin liner.

Cream the butter and sugar in a bowl with an electric hand mixer. Add the eggs, one at a time, mixing well after each addition. Add the vanilla extract and beat again briefly. Sift the flour and baking powder into a bowl, then gradually add to the creamed butter and sugar and beat again until well combined. Beat in the mashed bananas and finally stir in the chocolate pieces.

Pour the mixture into the loaf tin and level it out with a spatula. Bake in the centre of the oven for 50 minutes, until a skewer inserted into the centre of the cake comes out clean. Leave the cake in the tin to cool.

This loaf cake is best served warm. Keep any uneaten cake in an airtight container at room temperature for about 3 days.

You will see a lovely combination of colours swirled together as you cut a slice of this marble loaf cake, which was always Lisa's birthday cake as she was growing up. It's best served soon after it comes out of the oven or at the very least on the day it is made.

MARBLE LOAF CAKE

150g unsalted butter, at room temperature, plus more for greasing tin
175g caster sugar
½ tsp good-quality vanilla extract
3 large eggs, free-range or organic
375g self-raising flour
¼ tsp salt
185ml milk
1 tbsp cocoa powder
Drop of red food colouring

Makes 1 x 900g loaf cake (8–10 slices)

Preheat the oven to 180°C/gas mark 4. Grease 1 x 900g loaf tin and line with baking paper or a loaf tin liner.

In a large bowl cream the butter and sugar together with an electric hand mixer until light and fluffy and then beat in the vanilla extract. Beat the eggs together in a small bowl or cup and then gradually add to the creamed butter and sugar and mix well.

Sift the flour and salt into in a bowl and gradually add to the batter, alternating with the milk and mixing well after each addition.

Divide the mixture between 3 bowls. Add the cocoa powder to one bowl and beat well, add the drop of red food colouring to another bowl and beat well, and leave the third bowl untouched.

Add alternate spoonfuls of each mixture to the tin, swirling them a little with a spatula or spoon as you go. Make sure the batter is evenly distributed and do a final swirl once all the mixtures are in.

Bake in the centre of the oven for 50–60 minutes – you may need to cover the top with a piece of foil for the last 10 minutes or so to stop the surface overcooking. When the cake is cooked, a skewer inserted into the centre should come out clean.

Allow the cake to cool in its tin for at least 10 minutes. Serve immediately after cooling, if possible. It can be kept in an airtight container or wrapped in clingfilm and stored at room temperature for 1–2 days only, as it tends to dry out more quickly than other sponges.

 **LOAVES AND SLICES**

LOAVES AND SLICES

A rich, sticky treat that you might find hard to stop eating once you start, this caramel slice is so moreish. When we used to supply it to Fernandez and Wells, an amazing café in London's Soho, we always made an extra one to serve in our shops.

CARAMEL SLICE

FOR THE BISCUIT BASE
200g plain flour, sifted
90g soft brown sugar
65g desiccated coconut
188g unsalted butter, melted,
  plus more for greasing tin

FOR THE CARAMEL FILLING
115g golden syrup
125g unsalted butter, broken or
  chopped into small pieces
2 x 397g tins condensed milk

FOR THE CHOCOLATE TOPPING
300g good-quality dark chocolate
  (at least 70% cocoa solids), broken
  into small pieces
2 tbsp corn oil
Cocoa powder, for dusting (optional)

Makes 12 pieces

Preheat the oven to 180°C/gas mark 4. Grease alarge rectangular baking tin. Line the base and the sides with baking paper and extend it above the sides so you can lift the whole slice out easily when it's ready.

To make the biscuit base, sift the flour and sugar into a bowl. Add the coconut and butter and mix together with an electric hand mixer until well combined. Press the mixture evenly and firmly into the baking tin. Bake for about 10–15 minutes, until golden brown. Do not overcook or it will have a tendency to break apart.

To make the caramel, put the golden syrup, butter and condensed milk into a saucepan over a low heat until the butter is completely melted. Continue cooking for 7–10 minutes as the caramel thickens and darkens in colour. Pour it over the prepared base and put back in the oven for 20 minutes.

Remove from the oven. Once it has completely cooled, prepare the chocolate topping by melting the chocolate and oil together very carefully either in a heatproof bowl set over a saucepan of simmering water or in a microsafe bowl in the microwave (heat for 1 minute, stir and heat for a further minute).

Pour the mixture over the caramel and smooth gently over the top. Allow to set before removing the whole slab from the tin and cutting into slices. You could sprinkle some cocoa powder over the top through a sieve just before serving.

The slices can be kept in an airtight container or clingfilm at room temperature for about 3 days.

LOAVES AND SLICES

Lamingtons originate from Australia and are small sponge squares dipped in either chocolate or jelly and then covered with coconut. They divide us all here at the bakery, between lovers or not of coconut, chocolate or pink, squares or fingers, cream or no cream. We make them for our New Zealand neighbour in Primrose Hill, Garry Trainer, who loves them whichever way they come.

Unlike most other cakes, Lamingtons taste better if they are made up when the sponge is a day old. Also they will be easier to make up if the sponge has been allowed to dry out a little and is not so fresh and crumbly. In fact you could leave it for longer than a day as it gets sturdier and easier to handle as it continues to dry out.

LAMINGTONS

2 batches Victoria sponge batter (see recipe for Victoria Sponge on page 98)
200g desiccated coconut
Butter, for greasing tin

FOR CHOCOLATE LAMINGTONS
2 tbsp unsalted butter
2 tbsp cocoa powder
6 tbsp boiling water
350g icing sugar
A few drops vanilla extract

FOR PINK LAMINGTONS
1 x 23g packet raspberry jelly
125ml boiling water
125ml cold water

FOR JAFFA LAMINGTONS
1 x 23g packet orange jelly
125ml boiling water
125ml cold water
1 tbsp cocoa powder

Makes 24 squares

Grease a large rectangular baking tin (a classic roasting tin would work just as well).

Make up a double batch of the Victoria sponge batter. Pour the batter into the prepared tin and level it out with a spatula. Bake in the centre of the oven for about 45 minutes, until the sponge is golden brown and a skewer inserted into the centre of the cake comes out clean.

Leave to cool in the tin for about 10 minutes and then turn out onto a wire rack to cool completely. Wrap the sponge in clingfilm and leave at room temperature for 24 hours or so, until you are ready to finish the Lamingtons.

When you are ready, preheat the oven to 180°C/ gas mark 4.

First you will need to cut the sponge into the desired shapes. Traditionally, a Lamington is cut into squares of about 5cm or rectangles of about 3 x 10cm. However, if you are making them for young children or you would prefer a smaller, canapé size, and you have left your sponge to well and truly dry out, then you could cut the shapes even smaller.

There are three variations of flavour, as detailed overleaf.

For Chocolate Lamingtons

Melt the butter in a heavy-based saucepan over a low heat. Dissolve the cocoa powder in the boiling water in a bowl and stir in the melted butter. Then mix in the icing sugar and vanilla extract and beat well.

For Pink Lamingtons

Dissolve the raspberry jelly in both the boiling water and cold water in a bowl. Leave to cool and set a little either at room temperature or in the fridge.

For Jaffa Lamingtons

Dissolve the orange jelly and the cocoa powder together in both the boiling water and cold water in a bowl. Leave to cool and set a little either at room temperature or in the fridge.

To assemble

Pour the desiccated coconut into a largish bowl. Using 2 forks as skewers, dip each sponge shape into your chosen flavour of liquid, making sure you coat all the sides as best you can. Let any excess liquid drip off while still holding the sponge piece over the bowl and then transfer the sponge to your coconut bowl. Remove the forks and use 2 fresh ones to roll the dipped sponge in the coconut to cover it completely. Place on a wire rack over a piece of baking paper to set.

The Lamingtons are now ready to serve. There is one final option available: you can split each one and fill with a little whipped cream and, if you have made the pink ones, a teaspoon of raspberry jam and a fresh raspberry.

The squares (without filling) can be kept in an airtight container or wrapped in clingfilm and stored at room temperature for about 3 days.

 **LOAVES AND SLICES**

  LOAVES AND SLICES

We don't make brownies very often, but this recipe was too good to leave out. It was devised by a former American chef of ours, Frances Money, who sadly has moved back to her home state of Texas. Her sunny character and great cooking skills are missed by all.

BROWNIES

**285g good-quality dark chocolate
(at least 70% cocoa solids), broken up**
**115g unsalted butter, plus more
for greasing tins**
450g light soft brown sugar
1 tsp salt
1½ tbsp instant espresso powder
6 large eggs, free-range or organic
1 tbsp good-quality vanilla extract
160g plain flour, sifted
1 tbsp baking powder
230g dark chocolate chips (optional)
**Icing sugar or cocoa powder, for dusting
(optional)**

Makes 12 squares

Preheat the oven to 150°C/gas mark 2. Grease a rectangular baking tin and line with baking paper.

Melt the chocolate and butter together, either in a heatproof bowl set over a saucepan of simmering water or in a microsafe bowl in the microwave (heat for 1 minute, stir, and then heat for a further minute, being careful not to burn it). Leave to cool.

Mix the sugar and espresso powder together in a large bowl. In a separate bowl, beat together the eggs and vanilla extract gently with an electric hand mixer. Add this egg mixture to the sugar mix and stir. Add the cooled chocolate and butter and mix again.

Finally, add the flour, baking powder and salt (and chocolate chips if using) and stir with a wooden spoon. Pour into the prepared tins, filling each tin to about two-thirds full and then level out the mixture with a spatula. Bake in the centre of the oven for about 30–40 minutes. You may need to shake or tap the oven rack that the tins are sitting on a couple of times during baking to knock out any excess air. It is important not to overcook brownies as they can dry out and they are much nicer when they are soft and gooey. The mixture will still cook a little when you take it out of the oven as it cools. Leave to cool in the tins.

If you want to cut it into squares, put it into the fridge for a while once it is cool, as you will find it is then much easier to cut cleanly. Dust with some icing sugar or cocoa before serving if desired.

LOAVES AND SLICES

Friands are little French cakes that have been lovingly adopted by the cafés and bakeries of Sydney, Australia. It was here, after a Saturday morning spent in the Paddington markets, that we tasted our first Friands and realised how good they were, especially with a traditional flat white coffee in hand. They couldn't be easier to make, and there is also potential for lots of different flavours, exchanging ingredients for another – we're sure, like us, you'll be trying different combinations in no time.

FRIANDS

FOR PEACH AND COCONUT FRIANDS

**100g unsalted butter, plus more
  for greasing tins**
100g good-quality white chocolate
230g desiccated coconut
345g icing sugar
115g plain flour
1 tsp good-quality vanilla extract
6 large egg whites, lightly beaten
3 peaches, chopped into small pieces
Icing sugar, for dusting (optional)

FOR RASPBERRY AND ALMOND FRIANDS

**200g unsalted butter, plus more
  for greasing tins**
115g plain flour
345g icing sugar
230g ground almonds
2 tsp good-quality vanilla extract
6 large egg whites, lightly beaten
230g fresh raspberries
Icing sugar, to dust (optional)

Makes 12

Grease 12 individual friand tins or mini loaf tins. Preheat the oven to 190°C/gas mark 5.

For Peach and Coconut Friands
Gently melt the butter and white chocolate together in a heavy-based saucepan, stirring continually.
 Sift all the dry ingredients into a mixing bowl and combine well. Add the remaining ingredients, except the peaches, and stir gently until just combined. Finally, add the chopped peaches on the top.
 Divide the mixture evenly between the prepared tins, filling them to just over half-full.

For Raspberry and Almond Friands
Melt the butter very gently in a heavy-based pan.
 Sift the flour and icing sugar into a bowl. Add the remaining ingredients, except for the raspberries, and stir until just combined. Stir in the melted butter and mix again.
 Divide the mixture evenly between the prepared tins, filling them to just over half-full. Top each tin with 3 or 4 raspberries.

To bake and finish Friands
Bake in the centre of the oven for 20–25 minutes. Leave to cool slightly in their tins for 5 minutes before turning out onto a wire rack to cool completely. Before serving, dust with a little icing sugar if you wish.
 The Friands will keep for 3 days in an airtight tin or wrapped in clingfilm and stored at room temperature.

This is another slice that was inspired by a wonderful recipe of Bill Granger's and we have been making it almost since the very beginning of Primrose Bakery. We used to make it on a very regular basis when we first started out by supplying cakes and cupcakes to the Melrose and Morgan delicatessen, which is located across the road from us in Primrose Hill.

For an autumnal seasonal alternative, you could replace the raspberries and raspberry jam with blackberries and blackberry jam.

COCONUT AND RASPBERRY SLICE

125g unsalted butter, plus more for greasing tin
60g golden caster sugar
1 large egg, free-range or organic
1 tsp good-quality vanilla extract
185g plain flour, sifted
1 tsp baking powder
60ml milk
200g good-quality raspberry jam
300g fresh raspberries

FOR THE TOPPING
100g unsalted butter, at room temperature
5 tbsp golden caster sugar
2 large eggs
225g desiccated coconut
60g plain flour

Makes 12 squares

Preheat the oven to 180°C/gas mark 4. Grease a large rectangular baking tin and line the base and sides with baking paper, extending the paper slightly over the sides of the tin.

In a bowl cream together the butter and sugar with an electric hand mixer. Add the egg and the vanilla extract and mix well. Slowly add the dry ingredients until well combined and then beat in the milk. This should give you a dough-like mixture. Put this in the prepared tin, then level out the top with a spatula and spread the raspberry jam on top.

To make the topping, cream the butter and sugar with an electric hand mixer and then beat in the rest of the ingredients to give you a mixture with quite a thick consistency. Spoon this over the jam in the tin, again ensuring it is evenly spread.

Bake in the centre of the oven for about 30 minutes, until cooked and golden brown on top and a skewer inserted into the centre of the slice comes out clean.

Allow to cool in the tin. Once it is cool, you can lift the whole slice out of the tin by lifting up the edges of the baking paper and then put it on a chopping board to cut into squares.

These will keep for 3 days in an airtight tin or wrapped in clingfilm and stored at room temperature.

One of our year-round bestselling cakes, although probably not strictly a 'cake', this is a very sweet, sticky treat that's hard to resist!

MARS BAR CAKE

**70g unsalted butter, plus more
   for greasing tin**
3 tbsp golden syrup
**6 Mars bars (standard size 58g bars),
   chopped into small pieces**
200g cornflakes

Makes 1 x 20cm round cake (approx.
10–12 slices)

Grease 1 x 20cm sandwich cake tin and line the base with baking paper.

Melt the butter and golden syrup gently in a heavy-based saucepan over a very low heat, stirring continuously. Add the chopped Mars bars and keep stirring until they have just melted. Remove from the heat and then gently fold in the cornflakes.

Spoon the mixture into the tin, pressing it down to distribute it evenly. Allow it to cool and set completely before serving, which will take about 1 hour. Remove from the tin, peel away the baking paper and cut into slices. It will inevitably be very sticky.

These will keep for 3 days in an airtight tin or wrapped in clingfilm and stored at room temperature.

 **LOAVES AND SLICES**

This rich dark chocolate tart is really more of a dessert than a cake, so we usually make a whole tart for a customer rather than sell it by the slice. It's delicious served with cream or vanilla ice-cream. This recipe was created for us by Jess Leefe, one of the first pastry chefs we employed when we opened our Primrose Hill shop. Jess was a huge asset to us and extremely talented.

DARK CHOCOLATE TART

FOR THE SWEET PASTRY (PÂTE SUCRÉE)
250g plain flour
70g golden caster sugar
150g unsalted butter, at room tempera-ture, plus more for greasing tin
2 large egg yolks, free-range or organic

FOR THE FILLING
330ml double cream
2 level tsp caster sugar
Pinch of salt
120g unsalted butter
455g good-quality dark chocolate (at least 70% cocoa solids)
120ml cold milk
Cocoa powder, for dusting

Makes 1 x 28cm round tart

First, make the sweet pastry by sifting together the flour and sugar, then place in the bowl of a food processor and add the butter and the egg yolks. Mix on full speed until the mixture comes together in large crumbs. (Be careful not to overmix as this can make the consistency of the dough very tough and chewy.)

Turn the pastry out onto a floured surface and flatten into a round disc, using your hands (make sure your hands are not too warm when doing this). Wrap in clingfilm and put in the fridge for at least 1 hour.

Preheat the oven to 180°C/gas mark 4. Grease a 28cm fluted flan tin with a removable base.

When you are ready to roll out the pastry, first flour the work surface. Then, rather than rolling back and forth over the pastry, gently push the rolling pin down to form little ridges – this prevents the pastry from cracking. Keep gently turning the pastry disc so that it does not stick to the work surface. You will need to roll it out to about 3mm thick (about the thickness of a 50p coin).

Carefully press the dough into the prepared tin and trim the edges back to the sides of the tin. Prick the base of the dough with a fork in a few different places, cover with a sheet of baking paper and weigh it down with some ceramic baking beans (or other dried beans). Bake in the centre of the oven for about 20 minutes, or until a light golden brown. Remove the beans and allow the pastry shell to cool completely in the tin.

To make the filling, combine the cream, sugar and salt in a large, heavy-based saucepan and bring to a boil. Remove from the heat and add the butter and chocolate. Stir until they are both completely melted and then allow the mixture to cool slightly. Add the milk and stir until the mixture is smooth and shiny.

Pour the mixture into the pastry shell. Shake the flan tin gently to even it out and then smooth the top with a spatula. Allow it to cool and set at room temperature for 1–2 hours. Dust with cocoa powder through a sieve. Any that is uneaten should be stored in the fridge, where it will keep for 2–3 days.

 LOAVES AND SLICES

 **LOAVES AND SLICES**

These are a New Zealand delicacy – or at least as far as Lisa is concerned, along with Pinky bars and her dad's beer-battered oysters! They are very simple to make, although how much time you spend on perfecting your icing finish is entirely up to you. Either way, they will taste delicious. Adding the pulp of a passion fruit to your icing and leaving off the chocolate half is a healthier alternative.

NEENISH TARTS

FOR THE TART SHELLS

250g plain flour
70g golden caster sugar
150g unsalted butter, at room
**   temperature, plus more for**
**   greasing tins**
2 large egg yolks, free-range or organic

FOR THE FILLING

125g unsalted butter, at room
**   temperature**
125g icing sugar, sifted
4 tbsp condensed milk
1 tbsp freshly squeezed lemon juice
Raspberry jam (allow ½ tsp per tart)

FOR THE ICING

3–4 tbsp unsalted butter, at room
**   temperature**
350g icing sugar, sifted
1 tbsp cocoa powder, sifted
2 tbsp boiling water
A few drops pink food colouring
**   (optional)**

Makes approx. 22 tarts

Make the tart shells first. Sift together the flour and sugar, then place in the bowl of a food processor and add the butter and the egg yolks. Mix on full speed until the mixture comes together in large crumbs. (Be careful not to overmix as this can make the consistency of the dough very tough and chewy.)

Turn the pastry out onto a floured surface and flatten into a round disc, using your hands (make sure your hands are not too warm when doing this). Wrap in clingfilm and put in the fridge for at least 1 hour.

As this recipe will give you quite a lot of tart shells, you can at this stage halve the dough, wrap one of the halves in clingfilm and freeze until needed. Alternatively, store it in the fridge if you are planning to use it in a few days' time.

Once you are ready to prepare the tarts, roll out the dough to a 5mm thickness on a floured work surface. We use a 5.5cm-diameter biscuit cutter to cut the circles from the dough, as this seems to work best with a standard tart tray (which is shallower than a muffin tray).

Preheat the oven to 180°C/gas mark 4. Grease as many tart tins as you need. Carefully place each circle of dough in the centre of each tart hole on the tray and press with your fingertips to shape it so that it fits the whole hole, allowing the edges of the dough to reach right to the top of the sides of the hole.

Cover the tray loosely with a sheet of baking paper and then fill each pastry shell with some ceramic baking beans. Once the shells are in the trays, rest them again in the fridge for a further 10 minutes.

Take the tray out of the fridge and bake the tart shells in the oven for about 10 minutes. Remove the beans and the baking paper and then put back in the oven for another 5 minutes, until the pastry is a light golden brown. Allow to cool completely.

To make the filling, put all the ingredients (remember to halve the quantities if using only half of the dough), except for the raspberry jam, in a bowl and beat well with an electric hand mixer until you have a thick creamy paste. Drop ½ teaspoon of raspberry jam into the centre of each tart shell. Then spoon some of the filling into each shell and spread evenly with a knife so that it fills the whole shell. Allow to set for about 1 hour at room temperature.

 LOAVES AND SLICES

For the icing, you will need to make 2 separate bowlfuls, one for the chocolate icing and the other for the pink icing (again, remember to halve the total ingredients if using only half the dough). In the first bowl beat half the butter, icing sugar, cocoa powder and water to a smooth finish. In the other bowl, beat the remaining butter, icing sugar, water and a drop or two of pink colouring (or you can leave this one uncoloured if preferred).

To finish the Neenish Tarts, first we usually ice the whole tart with a thin layer of pink icing. Then, to ensure a neat finish, we use a piping bag (see page 224) filled with the chocolate icing to draw a line across the centre of the tart and then fill in one half with some more of the chocolate icing.

Any uneaten tarts will keep in an airtight container at room temperature for 2–3 days

LOAVES AND SLICES

Milo is a chocolate and malt powder, originally from Australia, where it was first produced in 1934, but is now easily found in the UK and, indeed, all over the world in its distinctive green tin. It's very similar to Ovaltine, which can be substituted in this recipe with an equally good result.

MILO CRUNCH

FOR THE BASE

250g plain flour

2 tsp baking powder

4 tbsp soft brown sugar

250g desiccated coconut

2½ tbsp Milo or Ovaltine powder,
  plus more for dusting

200g unsalted butter, plus more
  for greasing tin

FOR THE ICING

50g unsalted butter

400g icing sugar, sifted

70ml water

Makes 12 pieces

Preheat the oven to 180°C/gas mark 4. Grease and line a large rectangular baking tin. It's a good idea to line the tin completely with the baking paper and extend it above the sides of the tin a little – you will then easily be able to lift the whole slice out when it is ready.

Start by making the base. Sift all the dry ingredients into a bowl and stir to combine. Melt the butter carefully in a heavy-based saucepan over a low heat, stirring continuously, then pour it into the bowl of dry ingredients and mix well. Press the dough evenly and firmly into the prepared tin. Bake in the oven for about 25 minutes, until golden brown. Allow to cool completely in the tin while you make the icing.

Melt the butter in a saucepan over a low heat and then combine it with the water and icing sugar in a bowl and beat well. The icing will have quite a liquid consistency.

Once the base has cooled, gently pour the icing over the whole surface and spread it out evenly with a spatula. Finish by dusting with some Milo or Ovaltine powder and cut into rectangular or square pieces as you wish.

These will keep for up to 3 days in an airtight container or wrapped in clingfilm and stored at room temperature.

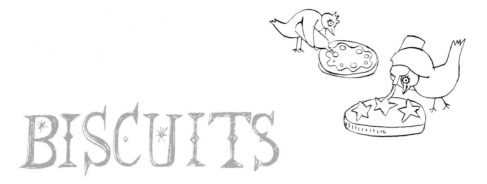

BISCUITS

Biscuits are a welcome addition to any afternoon tea or simply with a cup of coffee when a cupcake or piece of cake seems too indulgent. Because of Lisa's New Zealand origins, our biscuits often have an Australian/New Zealand slant to them and they have proved amazingly popular. They are less fragile than our cupcakes so are a little easier to transport to picnics. Wrapped in cellophane and tied with a ribbon, they also make great presents.

This is one of our favourite and oldest recipes. It belonged to Martha's Great-Aunt Mary and has been passed down through the family and kept carefully by Martha's Uncle John, reaching us still on the original handwritten piece of paper.

AUNT MARY'S BOURBON BISCUITS

FOR THE BISCUITS

225g unsalted butter, at room temperature
225g golden caster sugar
4 heaped tsp golden syrup
340g self-raising flour
115g cornflour
115g cocoa powder
4 tbsp water, or more if needed

FOR THE ICING

2 tbsp cocoa powder
4 tsp warm water
115g unsalted butter, at room temperature
6 tbsp icing sugar
½ tsp good-quality vanilla extract (optional)

Makes approx. 40 circles, to give 20 finished biscuits

To make the biscuits, cream the butter, sugar and golden syrup together in a bowl, using an electric hand mixer. Sift the flour, cornflour and cocoa powder together and beat into the creamed mixture, along with the water. If the mixture seems very dry, add a little more water. Knead thoroughly to form a smooth thick dough. You can either rest the dough in the fridge until you are ready to finish making the biscuits, or roll it out straight away.

Once you are ready, preheat the oven to 180°C/gas mark 4. Line a baking tray with baking paper.

Lightly flour a work surface and roll out the dough to a thickness of 3–4mm. Using a circular 5cm biscuit cutter, cut into about 40 circles.

Lay each circle on the tray, leaving a little space between. Bake in the oven for 10–12 minutes, until hard to the touch. Make sure you don't overcook them or they will burn. Allow to cool.

To make the icing, sift the cocoa powder into a bowl, add the warm water, and stir together. In a separate bowl, beat the butter until smooth, using an electric hand mixer, add the icing sugar and vanilla extract (if using) and beat well. Add the cocoa and warm water.

Sandwich 2 biscuits together with a thin layer of the chocolate icing and when they are all iced, dust with icing sugar. These biscuits are best eaten on the day they are baked, but will keep for 2–3 days in an airtight biscuit tin.

SAUSAGE DOG BISCUITS

Makes 25–30 biscuits, depending on size and shape of cutter

As an alternative to the classic round Bourbon Biscuits on the previous page, you could use any shaped biscuit cutter, animal or otherwise, to produce a thin chocolate biscuit and then decorate as you wish. We make sausage dog biscuits because of Martha's dachshund, Charlie, who is a regular visitor to our Primrose Hill shop, and in fact as a tribute to all the many sausage dogs that seem to live in and around Primrose Hill. These biscuits are great fun to decorate with icing collars, noses, tails, ears and some are even known
to sport a bikini. Just make sure you don't feed them to your dog!

Preheat the oven to 180°C/gas mark 4. Make up the dough according to the recipe for Aunt Mary's Bourbon Biscuits on the previous page and roll it out on a floured work surface to a thickness of about 4mm. Then cut out your desired shapes, place on a baking sheet lined with baking paper and bake for 8–9 minutes, until firm to the touch but not beginning to blacken.

Allow to cool fully before icing or decorating. These are best eaten on the day they are made, but will keep for 2–3 days in an airtight tin or wrapped in clingfilm.

A favourite Canadian biscuit, these are a recent addition to our range and are made for us by our Canadian chef, Julia. Our customers seem to never tire of ginger-flavoured biscuits, cakes and cupcakes, so these always get quickly snapped up!

GINGER SNAP BISCUITS

170g unsalted butter, at room temperature
200g granulated sugar
1 large egg, free-range or organic, beaten
85g black treacle/molasses
250g plain flour, sifted
1 tsp bicarbonate of soda
1 tsp ground cinnamon
½ tsp ground cloves
1 tsp ground ginger
100g granulated sugar, for coating

Makes 25–30 biscuits

In a large bowl cream together the butter, sugar, egg and treacle, using an electric hand mixer, until well combined. Mix in the remaining ingredients, until the mixture comes together in a dough. Place in the fridge for about 1 hour.

When ready to roll out the biscuits, preheat the oven to 180°C/gas mark 4. Line 2 baking trays with baking paper.

Take the dough out of the fridge and carefully roll tablespoonfuls of the dough into small balls. Place the granulated sugar in a bowl and dip each ball into the sugar, then sprinkle with 2–3 drops of cold water (which will give the biscuits a 'cracked' effect once they have been cooked).

Place the balls on the prepared baking trays, leaving a space of about 5cm between each one as they will increase in size as they cook. Bake in the oven for 10–12 minutes, until the edges of the biscuits have hardened but the centre remains soft.

Remove from the oven and transfer to a wire rack to cool. The finished biscuits should be crunchy on the outside and chewy on the inside. These biscuits are best eaten the same day, but will keep for 2–3 days in an airtight tin or wrapped in clingfilm and stored at room temperature.

 BISCUITS

Melting Moments are the heirs to custard creams. Those poor Australian descendants of English stock must have adapted the first recipe in homage to the British teatime biscuit. When Lisa was a child, her mother would bake them in the heat of the Australian Christmas holidays and store them in the freezer. She and her brother discovered just how good they were to eat straight from the freezer, without ever restoring them to their rightful room temperature!

MELTING MOMENTS

FOR THE BISCUITS

200g unsalted butter, softened
190g icing sugar, plus more for dusting
155g plain flour
140g cornflour
½ tsp baking powder

FOR THE FILLING

2 tbsp custard powder
100g unsalted butter, at room temperature
150g icing sugar, sifted
2–3 tbsp water

Makes approx. 24 discs, to give 12 finished biscuits

Preheat the oven to 180°C/gas mark 4. Line 2 baking trays with baking paper.

For the biscuits, sift all the dry ingredients together in a bowl, add the butter and mix well with an electric hand mixer.

Using your hands, roll tablespoonfuls of the mixture into about 24 small balls. Place the balls on the baking trays, leaving a space of about 5cm between each one. Gently press down on the top of each biscuit with a fork to flatten them so they are almost doubled in size.

Bake for about 9 minutes, until they are a light golden brown. Don't overcook them or they will become too crispy.

For the custard filling, mix the custard powder, butter and icing sugar in a bowl, using an electric hand mixer, and gradually add the water until the desired spreading consistency is reached.

Using an icing spatula or a flat-edged knife, spread a small amount of icing on the flat side of a biscuit and sandwich together with another biscuit. Repeat with the remaining biscuits and dust with icing sugar, to finish.

These are best eaten on the same day they are baked, but will keep for 2–3 days in an airtight tin or wrapped in clingfilm and stored at room temperature.

BISCUITS

Afghan biscuits are a traditional Australian treat, and the nation's favourite biscuit. The combination of such simple ingredients should not taste this good – but it does! The name often invites curiosity over its origin: we have found links to WW1 soldiers' helmets, Afghan hounds, good-luck walnuts, and more.

AFGHAN BISCUITS

FOR THE BISCUITS

200g unsalted butter, at room temperature
75g golden caster sugar
175g plain flour, sifted
25g cocoa powder, sifted
50g cornflakes

FOR THE TOPPING

1 batch Chocolate Buttercream Icing (see recipe overleaf)
3–4 walnuts, cut in half, to decorate

Makes 6–8 biscuits

Preheat the oven to 180°C/gas mark 4. Line a baking tray with baking paper.

In a bowl cream the butter and sugar together with an electric hand mixer, until the mixture is pale and fluffy. Gradually add the flour and cocoa powder and beat again. Lastly, add the cornflakes and stir in with a spoon until combined.

Put approximately 2 tablespoonfuls each of the mixture in neat piles on the baking tray, leaving a little space between each one, and flatten them slightly with the back of a fork. Bake in the oven for about 15 minutes, or until just becoming firm to the touch. Allow to cool slightly on the tray and then transfer to a wire rack.

When the biscuits are completely cool, use a spatula or a flat-edged knife, to spread a small amount of the Chocolate Buttercream Icing on top of each biscuit and decorate each one with 1–2 walnut halves.

These biscuits will keep for 2–3 days in an airtight tin or wrapped in clingfilm and stored at room temperature.

CHOCOLATE BUTTERCREAM ICING

**175g good-quality dark chocolate
(at least 70% cocoa solids)**
**115g unsalted butter, at room
temperature**
125g icing sugar, sifted
½ tbsp semi-skimmed milk
½ tsp good-quality vanilla extract

Makes enough to ice 6–8 biscuits

Melt the chocolate either in a heatproof bowl set over a pan of simmering water or in a microsafe bowl in the microwave, until the chocolate is smooth and has a thick pouring consistency. (If using a microwave, heat on a medium heat for 1 minute, stir and then heat for a further minute, taking care not to burn the chocolate.) Leave to cool slightly.

In a bowl beat the butter, sugar, milk and vanilla together until smooth. Add the melted chocolate and beat until thick and creamy.

This icing can be stored in an airtight container at room temperature for up to 3 days. Remember to beat well before reusing. If it looks too runny to use to ice the biscuits, simply keep beating – this will thicken the icing and improve its consistency.

  BISCUITS

We love these cookies when they are only just cooked, still warm and not too crispy apart from the crunchy caster sugar dusted on their tops.

PEANUT BUTTER COOKIES

285g plain flour
¾ tsp bicarbonate of soda
½ tsp baking powder
¼ tsp salt
115g unsalted butter, at room temperature
230g crunchy peanut butter
175g golden caster sugar, plus more for dusting
115g light soft brown sugar
1 large egg, free-range or organic
1 tbsp milk
1 tsp good-quality vanilla extract
230g peanut butter chips (or 230g unsalted peanuts if you can't find the chips)

Makes 20–24 cookies

Preheat the oven to 180°C/gas mark 4. Line 2 baking trays with baking paper.

Sift the first 4 ingredients together in a bowl. In a separate bowl beat the butter and peanut butter until smooth, then beat in the sugars. Add the egg, milk and vanilla extract and beat again. Add the dry ingredients and, finally, the peanut butter chips or unsalted peanuts and mix until everything is incorporated and the mixture comes together as a dough. Using your hands, bring the dough together into a large ball and place on the work surface. You do not need to roll it out before starting to make each cookie.

Weigh out 40g of dough per cookie, which is about 2 tablespoons, and roll into a ball with your hands. Place the balls, spaced out, on the baking tray and press down gently on each one with the back of a fork to flatten them slightly. Bake for 10 minutes, until they just begin to firm up. Do not overcook or they will be very crisp.

While the cookies are still warm, lightly dust each one with a little golden caster sugar. Leave to cool slightly on the tray, then transfer to a wire rack to cool completely. Store any uneaten cookies in an airtight container at room temperature for 3–4 days.

If you don't want to bake the cookies straight away, you can store this dough in the fridge – but don't keep it for more than a week. Or you could freeze the unused dough for up to 2 months.

These crunchy, nutty cookies are even more delicious when you make them with our granola – and even more impressive to show off to your friends.

GRANOLA AND WHITE CHOCOLATE COOKIES

460g plain flour
1 tsp bicarbonate of soda
½ tsp salt
230g unsalted butter, at room temperature
115g granulated sugar
115g soft light brown sugar
1 large egg
1 tsp good-quality vanilla extract
230g granola, home-made (see recipe on page 93) or ready-made
230g almonds, coarsely chopped
150g good-quality white chocolate, roughly chopped

Makes 20–24 cookies

Preheat the oven to 180°C/gas mark 4. Line 2 baking trays with baking paper.

Sift the flour, bicarbonate of soda and salt into a bowl, combine well and set aside. In a separate, large bowl cream the butter and sugars together with an electric hand mixer. Add the egg and vanilla extract and beat well, then gradually add the flour mixture, mixing well after each addition. Using a spoon, stir in the granola, almonds and white chocolate until all is well combined. The mixture should come together in a dough, from which you can start measuring out your cookies, without any need to roll out.

Weigh out 30–35g dough per cookie, which is just less than 2 tablespoons, and roll into a ball with your hands. Place the balls, spaced out, on the baking tray and press down gently on each one with the back of a fork, to flatten them slightly. Bake for 9–10 minutes, until they begin to firm up.

If you don't want to bake the cookies straight away, you can store the unused dough, wrapped in clingfilm, in the fridge for up to a week, or freeze it for up to 2 months.

Store any uneaten biscuits in an airtight tin at room temperature for 3–4 days.

  BISCUITS

We have been making these biscuits for so long now that we felt we should include them in this chapter. However, we must give full credit to Nigella Lawson here, as they first came to our attention via her *How to be a Domestic Goddess* cookbook and have been very slightly tweaked by us since then. We find countless occasions to have an excuse to bake these, with so many fantastic cutters to be found – which we both look out for on our travels – and colours to be used.

ICED BISCUITS

FOR THE BISCUITS

85g unsalted butter

100g golden caster sugar

1 large egg, free-range or organic

½ tsp good-quality vanilla extract

200g plain flour, sifted, plus more for rolling

½ tsp baking powder

¼ tsp salt

FOR THE ICING

150g icing sugar

2–3 tbsp boiling water, or as needed

A few drops food colouring

Makes approx. 30 biscuits, depending on size of cutter used

Preheat the oven to 180°C/gas mark 4. Line 1 or 2 baking trays with baking paper.

Cream the butter and sugar together in a bowl, and then add the egg and mix well. Gradually add the flour, salt, and baking powder and mix.

On a floured work surface roll the dough out to a thickness of about 5mm, then cut into your desired shapes and place, well spaced out, on the baking tray(s). Bake for about 10–12 minutes, until the biscuits are a light golden brown. They will cook quickly – so keep an eye on the cooking time – and will continue to cook a little once they are out of the oven. Leave to cool on a wire rack.

To make up the icing, sift the icing sugar into a bowl and add about 1 tablespoonful of boiling water at a time. Beat well to a thick but still liquid consistency. If you add too much water, simply add more icing sugar. Add 1 drop of food colouring at a time.

When you are ready to ice the biscuits, lay them out on a flat work surface. If you want the icing to have a perfect finish, it is best to use a piping bag to pipe an outline around the biscuits and allow to dry, then fill in the remainder with a slightly thinner consistency of icing. For details, wait until the base coat is dry to the touch, then use a piping bag with a different colour icing. If decorating with sprinkles or sweets, this is best done when the icing is still a bit damp.

These will keep for 2–3 days in an airtight tin or wrapped in clingfilm and stored at room temperature.

Icing biscuits is one of Lisa's favourite tasks and the results are certainly amazing (which she herself would be happy to admit!) and these gingerbread men and camels fill our shop throughout December, all individually adorned. Don't worry if you don't have a gingerbread man biscuit cutter, you can use any cutter. Be as creative as you like when decorating them.

GINGERBREAD MEN AND CAMELS

75g soft dark brown sugar
50g golden syrup
25g black treacle/molasses
1 tsp cinnamon
1 tsp ginger
Pinch of cloves
Pinch of ground nutmeg
Rind of ½ orange
95g unsalted butter
225g plain flour, sifted, plus more
  for rolling
½ tsp bicarbonate of soda
Royal or water icing, from a packet
  or home-made (see icing instructions
  in recipe for Iced Biscuits on previous
  page, adjusting the quantities as
  needed)

Makes approx. 15 biscuits

Put the brown sugar, golden syrup, black treacle, spices and orange rind into a heavy-based saucepan over a high heat until the sugar is dissolved, which should take about 3–5 minutes.

Remove the pan from the heat and stir in the butter until it is completely melted. Stir in the flour and bicarbonate of soda until a soft dough is formed. Wrap the dough in clingfilm and refrigerate for at least 1 hour, or overnight.

To cook the biscuits, preheat the oven to 180°C/gas mark 4. Line 1–2 baking trays with baking paper. Roll the dough out onto a large, flat, floured work surface to a thickness of about 2mm. Carefully cut out the shapes with the biscuit cutter and then place on the baking tray(s), leaving a little space between each.

Bake for 8–10 minutes. To test if they are cooked, feel the centre of one – it should feel stiff but not hard. The edges must not be too dark, otherwise it will be brittle and bitter.

Allow the biscuits to cool fully before icing. Ideally, use royal or water icing, and use a different-coloured icing for creating the eyes and mouth. We also find the tubes of Silver Spoon Designer Icing very good for this kind of decorating.

Allow the icing to set a little before serving. They also make great presents – you can wrap them individually in a cellophane bag and tie with a ribbon. Alternatively, you could put a small hole in each before baking and turn them into hanging decorations with a small ribbon.

These biscuits will keep well in an airtight tin at room temperature for 3 or 4 days.

 **BISCUITS**

  **BISCUITS**

  BISCUITS

 BISCUITS

Delicate in both flavour and colour, these biscuits are a huge contrast to the giant, chocolate-chunk filled cookie that has dominated the 'cookie scene' in recent years. Of course there is a rightful place for all of them, although we think these dainty, rose-scented biscuits are the perfect addition to a special afternoon tea, alongside cucumber sandwiches, mini cupcakes and your favourite tea. Or you could make them for, say, a baby shower or give as a present.

ROSE BISCUITS

85g unsalted butter, at room temperature
100g golden caster sugar
1 large egg, free-range or organic
1 tbsp rose water
200g plain flour, plus more for rolling
1½ tsp baking powder
¼ tsp salt
1 batch Rose Water Icing (see recipe overleaf)
Crystallised rose petals, to decorate

Makes approx. 15 finished biscuits

Note: if you are using different-sized biscuit cutters, the cooking time will vary. Put similar-sized biscuits on the same tray so that you can keep an eye on the cooking times as smaller ones will bake faster and need to be removed from the oven sooner than larger ones.

Using an electric hand mixer, beat the butter and sugar in a bowl until pale and creamy. Add the egg and the rose water and beat again. In a separate bowl sift the flour, baking powder and salt together. Add this to the butter and sugar and beat gently until well combined. The resulting dough should not be too sticky, which would make it difficult to roll out – if it is, add more flour, just a tiny amount at a time.

Gather your dough into a single shape, wrap in clingfilm and put in the fridge to rest for 1 hour.

When you are ready to make the biscuits, preheat the oven to 180°C/gas mark 4 and line 2 baking trays with baking paper.

On a floured work surface, roll out the dough to a thickness of about 5mm. You may need to add a little more flour. Using a circular biscuit cutter, about 5.5cm in diameter, cut out as many biscuits as you can, putting the cutter close to each cut-out biscuit, so as not to waste any dough. You can gather up any remaining dough and roll again until it is used up.

Place the biscuits on the baking trays, about 1cm apart. Bake for 10–12 minutes until golden brown. Once they are cooked, transfer them to a wire rack and allow to cool fully before icing and assembling.

When they are cool, sandwich 2 biscuits together with a thin layer of icing in the middle and another layer on the top. Finish with a crystallised rose petal.

Any uneaten biscuits will keep for 2–3 days in an airtight container at room temperature.

ROSE WATER ICING

450g icing sugar
1 tsp rose water
About 6 tbsp hot water
Pink food colouring (optional)

Makes enough to ice 15 biscuits

Note: different varieties of rose water vary in strength.
We recommend a strong one, Star Kay White, available
from Waitrose. If you use a weaker one, remember to
increase the quantities recommended above to achieve
the same taste.

Sift the icing sugar into a bowl, add the rose water and then beat in enough hot water to make a stiff paste. If using colouring, add a drop or two to the icing and beat again. This should be plenty to give a beautiful pale pink colour.

These biscuits take us right back to the very early days of Primrose Bakery, when Lisa used to make them on an almost daily basis and in every conceivable shape and size for the delicatessen Melrose and Morgan. In the end we could hardly bear to look at, let alone eat, any but when we started to prepare the recipes for this book, we remembered how delicious they were, especially served with a cup of the Mariage Frères Earl Grey tea that we serve in our shops.

SHORTBREAD

125g icing sugar, sifted
225g plain flour, sifted, plus more
 for dusting
125g cornflour, sifted
225g unsalted butter, plus more
 for greasing tin
A little caster sugar, for sprinkling

Makes 12–15 bars

Preheat the oven to 180°C/gas mark 4. Grease a large rectangular baking tin.

Sift the icing sugar, flour and cornflour into the bowl of a food processor. Add the butter and beat on a slow speed until the mixture comes together. It should have the consistency of a pastry-like dough. Take the dough out of the bowl and, on a floured work surface, knead until it comes together in a large ball, but be very careful not to overmix or over-knead or it will dry out when baking.

Press the dough into the prepared tin, making sure it is evenly distributed throughout the tin. Mark the surface with a tip of a knife into the shapes of the biscuits you want after it has been baked, as this will help when you come to cut them out later. Prick the shortbread all over with a fork and bake for about 30 minutes. It's very easy to overcook shortbread, so keep an eye on it during cooking and as soon as it starts to turn golden brown around the edges of the tin, it should be ready to take out. It will continue to crisp up once it is out of the oven.

Sprinkle some caster sugar all over the shortbread and then allow it to cool in the tin. Once it is cool, cut out the biscuits, using the marked surface as a guide-line.

Store any uneaten shortbread in an airtight tin, where it should keep well for 5–7 days. Alternatively, you can freeze the cooked shortbread for up to 2 weeks and then defrost later.

  BISCUITS

WEDDING CAKES

In recent years, there has been an increasing trend to have tiers of cupcakes at a wedding rather than the traditional tiers of fondant-covered fruit cakes. You can use any flavour of cupcake for a wedding or large celebration and make a beautiful centerpiece. We make lots of wedding cakes like this and have catered for a huge range of events, from small, intimate gatherings to massive parties offering hundreds of different cakes. Some people prefer a very simple, elegant overall look while others want a complete mix of flavours and colours.

The versatility of cupcakes lies behind their popularity as wedding cakes – you really can cater for any type of wedding and they will always fit in brilliantly.

One of the added bonuses of our job is that we have visited many different venues while delivering and setting up wedding cakes and have felt privileged to be a part of so many people's special days, while having the chance to see many beautiful buildings, restaurants, flowers, table settings, and so on.

In our *Cupcakes* book we illustrated two very different looks for a tier of wedding cupcakes. Readers seem to have found this very helpful and it has provided them with inspiration for their own wedding cakes, whether made by us or by themselves.

Here we show some more ideas for possible ways of displaying them and for using different colours and flavours.

It's customary, though not essential, to have a small cake on the top level of the tier for cutting, and it can finish the whole display very well. First decide on your flavour of sponge – usually chocolate or vanilla – and the size, which will probably be 18cm or 20cm in diameter to fit the top plate of the tier. For the icing, we tend to use cream or another pale, pastel shade of vanilla buttercream – this seems to go well with most colour/flavour schemes on the tiers below but you could, of course, use any flavour.

Icing the top cake will take a little more time and care than many cakes as it really has to be perfect, so follow our step-by-step guide to achieve a beautiful finish.

 **WEDDING CAKES**

WEDDING CAKES

Step-By-Step Guide
to Icing a Layer Cake All Over

Once you have read 'How to Ice a Layer Cake' in the Tips and Techniques chapter, you can go a step further with our guidelines below on how to ice the top cake for a wedding tier.

1. Follow steps 1 and 2 on page 222, but use a bit more icing in the middle layer and this time push it out to the edges so that some starts to fall down the sides of the cake. The icing that actually covers the top of this bottom layer of cake should not be too thick – a thin layer is best.

2. With a smaller icing spatula or knife, work the buttercream right down to the base of this cake, turning the cake as you go in order to cover the whole of it so there is no sponge visible anywhere. Do not worry about neatness at this point or if a few crumbs creep through the icing.

3. Carefully position the second cake on top, pressing it down firmly in place. Make sure that it is centred and that there is not too much buttercream between the layers. Take 3–4 large spoonfuls of buttercream and start icing the top, again pushing the icing with your spatula out towards and over the edges. Spread the buttercream right down to meet the lower layer of icing on the sides so that eventually all the cake is covered. It doesn't matter about the finish at this stage.

4. At this point you may realise that there are too many crumbs visible through the icing. If so, simply smooth and scrape the icing so you are left with the minimal amount of coverage and put the cake into the fridge for about 15 minutes. Once the icing has set, it will hold all existing and future crumbs at bay and leave the surface smooth for you to continue with the icing. The thinner the layer of icing on the cake when you put it into the fridge, the faster it will set and the more effective it will be when you start icing again.

5. Once you have removed the cake from the fridge, start icing again immediately. Take about 4 large spoonfuls of buttercream and put it onto the centre of the top layer of cake. Spread it outwards, keeping it as evenly distributed as possible, and work to the sides and beyond. As it starts to fall over the sides push it down and around, but don't make it too thick or it will become too heavy for the sponge to withstand.

6. Decide what kind of finish you would like on the sides of the cake – smooth or textured. If you want a textured finish, try making some swirls through the icing. For a smoother finish, gently scrape all the sides, removing the excess (but not too much!) buttercream.

7. Once the sides are finished, scrape some of the icing from around the top edges of the cake back towards the centre of the cake and create some big swirls in the middle – you may need to add a little more icing to achieve this. Experiment with what you think looks best.

8. As a final step, clean the cake board very carefully with some paper towel, removing any icing that is on the board and tidying the bottom edge where the cake meets the board.

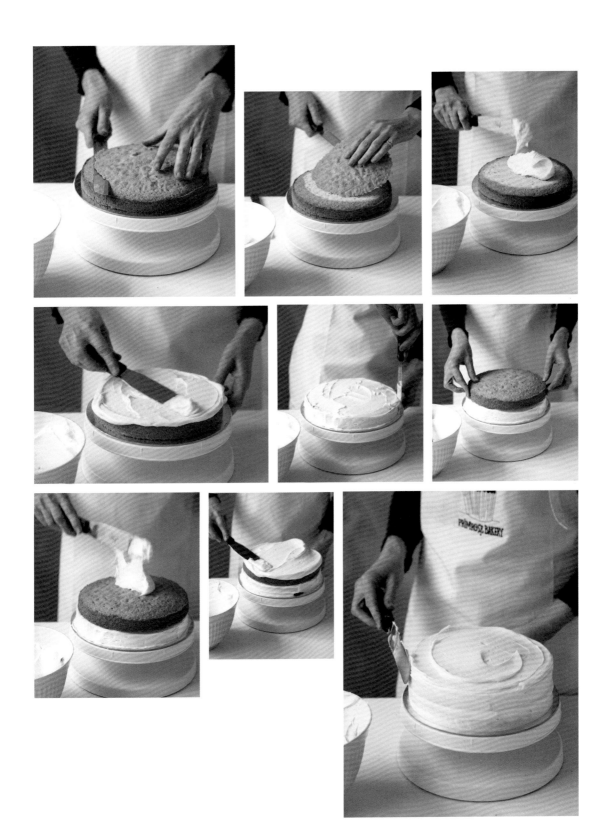

WEDDING CAKES

WEDDING CAKES

You are now ready to decorate the cake. It is probably best to coordinate the decorations for the top cake with those you are using on the cupcakes on the tiers below, to keep a consistent overall look. Fresh flowers on the top cake (and the tier) are always a bonus. More often than not we use roses, but many other types of flowers would work well too – ask the florist to make up a small posy to place in the centre or just keep a few stems back and break the stalks quite close up to the flower head before arranging prettily in the centre of the cake. Keep any fresh flowers in water until as close as possible to the time when the cake will be on show – this ensures the flowers will not wilt before it is cut.

For displaying your wedding cupcakes, there is now a wide selection of tiered cake stands available. In the Stockists section (see page 230) we have listed a couple of websites that we have found particularly useful and there is also usually a big choice available to buy through eBay.

We think the cupcakes look best if they are quite tightly packed on the tier, so it's a good idea to work out how many cakes you will have before deciding on the size of tier. If you are having a top cake, make sure it's a tier with a completely flat top plate, with none of the dividers or the spine of the tier coming through, otherwise the cake will not sit flat. In terms of size, you would usually need either a 10cm, 13cm or 20cm top cake to enable you to have at least 2 other layers underneath.

We mostly use Perspex tiers, which are completely clear and therefore do not detract from the overall look of the cake. They can usually be adjusted to correspond to the numbers of cakes, by either taking away or adding levels. However, they are a little fragile, so extreme care should be taken not to drop them as they tend to snap. For this reason it's also advisable to set up your wedding cake on a table in the spot where it will be displayed and therefore not have to be moved, to avoid any accidents!

There are many other types of tiers so it's down to individual taste and what works best in the room where the wedding will be held. For a smaller, budget wedding there are now some attractive cardboard stands on the market, available in a range of different colours and patterns and these look sensational when they are set up. We stock a lovely range of these, which come all the way from Australia where they are made by a woman who has set up her own small business – her husband is a pilot for Qantas and flies the A380 planes over to London from Sydney, often bringing with him a box of brightly coloured tiers for us in his hand luggage!

The most important thing to remember with a wedding cake, or indeed any celebration cake, is to take pleasure from making, displaying and eating it and not to worry unduly about any aspect of it, especially on what can otherwise be a very stressful occasion to organise.

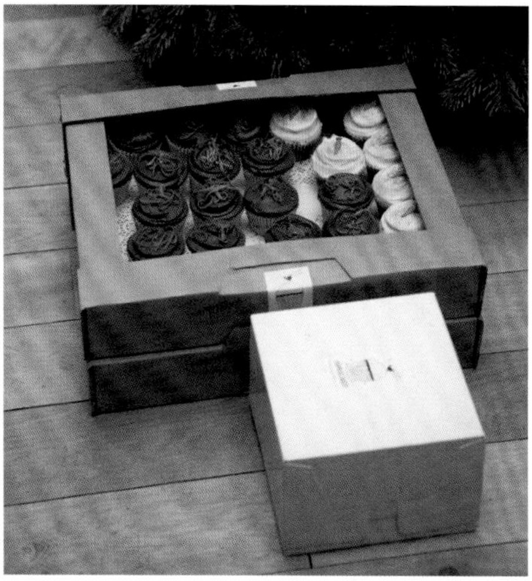

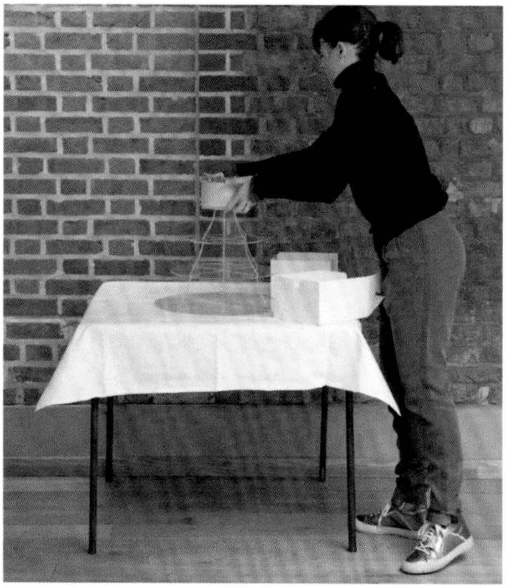

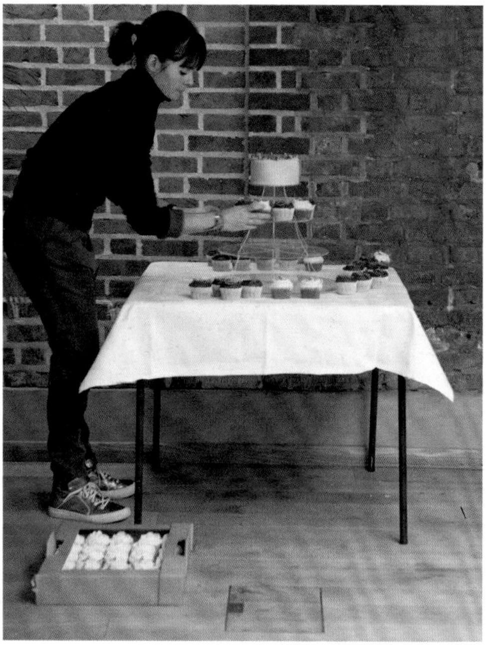

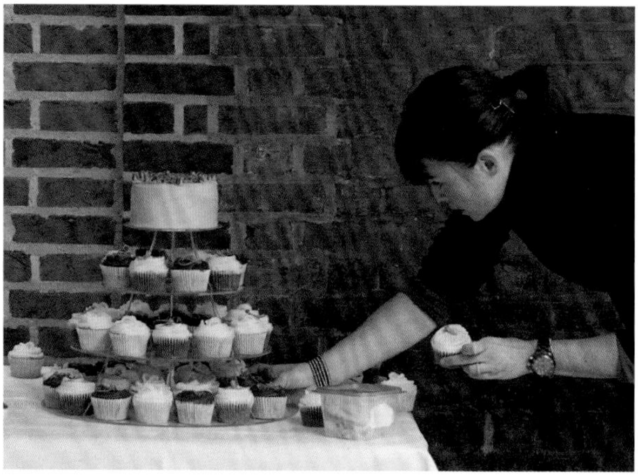

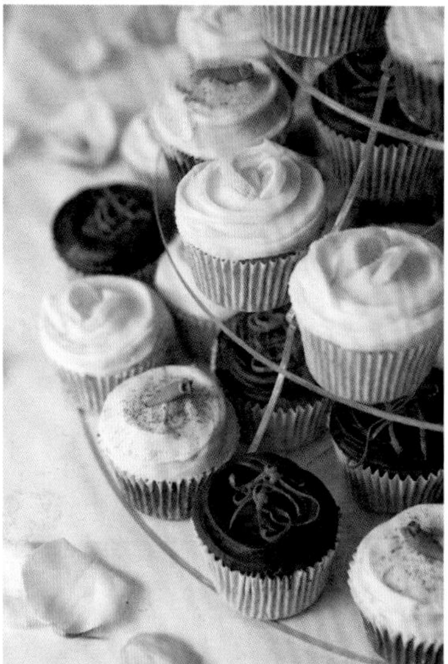

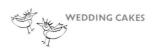

TECHNIQUES AND TIPS

In the seven years we have been baking, we have found a few techniques and tips that always help us ensure the best-tasting and -looking cupcakes, cakes, biscuits and so on. We are really happy to share them with you, although do remember that everyone will do things slightly differently, be working in different kitchens and have access to different equipment and ingredients. Never be afraid to give other things a go, but here is what is really important to us.

We have always stressed the importance of good-quality, seasonal ingredients in our baking as it really does make such a difference to the taste and the look of the finished product.

In our bakeries we try to only use fruit when it's in season in the UK or, at most, simply brought in from Europe. On the grounds of taste, cost and environmental concerns, we try not to use fruit that has had to travel from across the world. Also we feel it's good to vary our cakes through-out the year and give our customers something to look forward to at different times of the year.

Along with seasonal fruits, we also take great care to source the best ingredients we can find and afford. We still buy a lot of our everyday ingredients from supermar-kets as they often stock the most varied choice and ranges of sugar, flour, jams, and so on. Using a high-quality jam with a high-fruit content, for example, will enhance the flavour of your plum cupcake, jam filled croissant or Victoria sponge.

There are a few specialist ingredients which you will need, and which are worth tracking down. These are available online, via mail order, and so they should be relatively easy to get hold of.

There are one or two ingredients for which we find that only one particular brand works for us – the most important of these is our icing sugar. We only use Tate and Lyle – no other icing sugar comes close in our opinion. Their other sugars are also of a very high quality.

We are often asked to make Red Velvet cupcakes, which have become extremely popular in the UK in recent years and are made by some other bakeries. The reason we don't make them is simply that they contain more food colouring than we feel happy using – each batch of cupcakes could contain anything from a half to a whole bottle of red food colouring. However, we have been experimenting with beetroot to see whether it can give the desired colour, so hopefully this might be something new for the future!

For our regular size cupcakes we use standard white muffin cases in a muffin tray, and for our mini cupcakes we use mini muffin cases in a mini muffin tray. There are varying sizes of cases available in different shops and from different brands, so if you stick to a muffin case, rather than a fairy cake or cupcake case, you should find that it will work out well.

We love to source unusual and unique decorations from around the world. We get a lot of pleasure from doing this – it certainly beats doing the paperwork – and each season and special occasion through-out the year brings squeals of delight when we find something new. However, it really is down to individual preference when it comes to decorating your own cakes and cupcakes. Nowadays there is so much more choice available than even a couple of years ago and many of the mainstream supermarkets sell fabulous sugar decora-tions. Not all decorations have to be edible and not all cakes need decorating – just experiment with whatever you think looks best and keep an eye out for interesting decorations wherever you are.

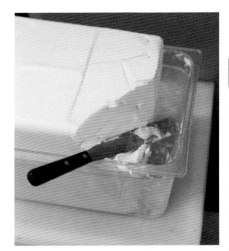

TECHNIQUES AND TIPS

How to Ice a Layer Cake

It's not difficult to achieve a visually stunning layer cake when working with buttercream icing. It can seem daunting, even to us, and we have iced cakes every day for the last seven years, but with practice and patience you will get the hang of it. (It makes us think of the techniques that bricklayers and plasterers use – those guys could make great cake icers!)

Icing a cake is very much a freehand thing, so the key is to experiment and you will come up with different results. Always allow yourself enough time to spend on icing the cake, as it's horrible to feel that you have to rush it and there's a time limit on finishing it.

Before starting, it's important that your chosen buttercream icing is of a very creamy, smooth consistency – so beat it very well, ideally with an electric hand mixer, and make sure it is at room temperature and not too cold or too hot. You can re-beat the icing as you go along, after you finish each step.

1. Place a silver cake board under one of the 2 cakes. It's a good idea to use a cake board that is 2 or 3cm bigger than the size of the cake – so for example, use a 23cm board for a 20cm cake. First, level the bottom layer of cake by using a serrated knife to even out the top, so you have a completely flat surface to work with. Gently pat the surface to brush off any crumbs, which will help make it easier to work with when you start icing.

2. Spread a couple of large spoonfuls of icing over this middle layer, using a spatula or flat-edged knife. Don't go right to the very edge of the cake, as the icing will be pushed out a little anyway when you place

TECHNIQUES AND TIPS

the other layer of cake on top. Make sure the icing is as evenly distributed as possible. Using this middle layer to practise icing is really helpful as you can do it as many times as you like, simply scraping it off in between until you feel confident about moving on to the top layer.

There are three different finishes you may want to achieve:

The swirl
The flat finish
The cake iced all over

The swirl

The swirl is a textured finish, much like the finish on one of our cupcakes, and so is perfect for decorating with sugar sprinkles or flowers.

1. A cake turntable is very helpful to achieve this finish as you will need to push the icing gently to the edges of the cake, ideally with a large icing spatula, working on a quarter of the surface at a time. To do this, you will need to keep turning the cake around as you move from one area to the next. Using about 2–3 tablespoons of icing, concentrate on getting the edges pretty and leave the centre until last.

2. Take one last big spoonful of icing, put it into the middle of the cake and, holding the spatula at a comfortable angle, push the icing lightly into a swirl. This will take a little practice, so smooth it over and start again if you want to and you are not under any pressure to finish quickly.

Always remember that you can scrape the icing off at any stage and start again. It is much better to spend more time and be happy with the end result rather than rush through it and then be disappointed.

The flat finish

A flat finish is required if you intend to pipe a message onto the cake.

1. Use the same amount of icing as for the swirl finish and cover the whole surface of the cake with the icing. The aim is to smooth the icing out evenly over the surface to make the finished icing very flat so that it creates the best surface to pipe the message on. Make sure you use enough icing, as with all the smoothing you don't want to end up with a bare patch!

2. Finish by tidying up the edges of the cake to get a neat finish with no icing overhanging the sides. Gently go round the edges with your icing spatula to make sure the icing just reaches as far as the edge of the sponge and the circle is even and tidy all the way round.

The cake iced all over

We have described the technique for icing the cake all over in the Wedding Cakes chapter (see page 212) as this method is most commonly used for the top cake of a wedding tier or for a christening or other special occasion.

Decorating

If you are planning on using sugar sprinkles for decoration, time will not be on your side when icing. The vanilla buttercream icing tends to set a little, making it hard for the sprinkles to stick, so you need to get them onto the cake as quickly as possible. However, chocolate buttercream does not set, and we recommend you use this while you are practising your technique, so that you can take your time to get the result you want.

Practice will make perfect with cake icing, but mistakes happen all the time, even for us in the bakery – we have been known to re-ice cakes at 8pm on a Saturday night after a 12- or 13-hour day to make sure they are perfect for any orders first thing on a Sunday morning or for one of our children's birthday cakes.

How to Make a Piping Bag

Buying disposable piping bags is easy enough, but often we make our own when using small amounts of icing that need lots of colours, and especially when using water icing to decorate biscuits.

1. Cut out a square piece of parchment or baking paper, about 30 x 30cm. Fold in half on the diagonal and cut into 2 pieces, to make 2 triangles. Each triangle will make one bag.

2. Take the 2 bottom corners of one triangle and cross them around and behind each other and then draw them up to align with the top corner. The thing to remember is that the resulting tip used for piping will actually be what was originally the centre point of the base of the triangle.

3. As you pull the corners up to meet the top corner, your triangle should have formed neatly into a cone shape. Gently pull the paper until the newly formed tip is fully closed, as if nothing could pass through it.

4. With your thumbs holding the cone firmly in place, make tiny folds from the top, outwards and down so that your paper cone feels secure and holds together on its own.

5. It is now ready to be filled with icing – fill it to about half-full so that you leave enough paper to fold in on itself to make it ready to use.

6. Finally, snip just the very end off to create your icing tip.

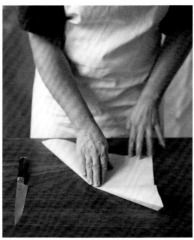

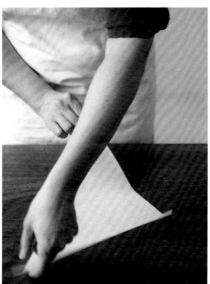

TECHNIQUES AND TIPS

Making Decorations from Sugarpaste

There are professional classes for this kind of thing and we are certainly not claiming to be sugar art experts, but thought we would share the basics of making your own sugar decorations. We've experimented ourselves over the last few years, making amongst other things Shrek ears and Donkey ears for the Everyman cinemas in London, where we supply cupcakes to match their latest feature films. So if you feel inclined to give it a go, here is a basic introduction to another whole area of cake decorating.

1. You can buy packets of ready-made sugarpaste in specialist food and party shops, some of which we've listed on our Stockists page at the back of the book. You can usually find it in blocks of different colours or just white, into which you can work a colour yourself if you need a particular shade. This requires a little time and a lot of kneading as you drop very small amounts of food colouring onto the block and work it through with your hands, adding more as you go, to reach the desired colour.

2. You may then need to roll the block out to the required thickness of your decoration or simply mould it directly from the block into shapes. There is an amazing range of tools and stencil cutters available to buy that can help with this task, or you can cut out a shape on some baking paper then lay it on the sugarpaste and cut around it. Just remember to wrap in clingfilm any sugarpaste you are not immediately working with as it will quickly become hard and all the kneading will have gone to waste!

3. When your creations are done, they should set quickly and become quite hard. You can then decorate your cake or cupcakes with them.

An alternative to colouring the sugarpaste would be to simply make the shapes in white and then paint over them with a little food colouring or some edible glitter. For the novice baker, this is a useful way of making simple shapes like footballs or other sporting decorations, small leaves, flowers, etc., or other very specialised decorations that might not be easy to buy ready-made.

STOCKISTS

Primrose Bakery
www.primrosebakery.org.uk
69 Gloucester Avenue, London NW1 8LD
Tel: 020 7483 4222
42 Tavistock Street, London WC2E 7PB
Tel: 020 7836 3638
Email: primrose-bakery@btconnect.com

www.cakescookiesandcraftsshop.co.uk
Decorations, equipment, wedding tiers

www.cakecraftworld.co.uk
Decorations, equipment, cupcake cases

Divertimenti
www.divertimenti.co.uk
Specialist baking equipment, tins, etc.

www.thedrinksshop.com
Violet syrup

Jane Asher party shop
www.janeasher.com
Decorations, baking tins, cases

John Lewis
www.johnlewis.com
Baking equipment, decorations

La Fromagerie
www.lafromagerie.co.uk
Violet syrup and violet sugar petals

Lakeland
www.lakeland.co.uk
Baking equipment, decorations

Marks and Spencer
www.marksandspencer.com
Ingredients, decorations, equipment

Partridges
www.partridges.co.uk
Specialist US ingredients

Rococo
www.rococochocolates.com
Sugared rose petals, violet petals, chocolates and sugared almonds for decorations

Selfridges
www.selfridges.com
Specialist ingredients

Squires Kitchen
www.squires-shop.com
Squires House, 3 Waverley Lane, Farnham,
Surrey GU9 8BB
Decorations, food colours

Waitrose
www.waitrose.com
Ingredients, decorations

The mixer used in the photography for
this book was supplied by KitchenAid
(www.kitchenaid.co.uk).

ACKNOWLEDGEMENTS

Primrose Bakery could not run without the dedication, hard work and passion of all its past and current staff. It's impossible to name everyone but they have all, in their own way, proved invaluable and we owe them huge thanks.

To our families we also owe thanks – particularly for their never-ending patience and understanding over our many, many hours spent away from home – Michael, Daisy and Millie Heath and Kevin, Thomas and Ned Thomas. And to our parents and siblings – Caroline Moorehead and Jeremy Swift, Daniel Swift, Camilla Swift, Roger and Marlene Glover, Martin and Kerrin Glover – who have all, in their own ways, been extremely supportive as our business has grown.

There are also many people who have helped us enormously with our business and books over the last seven years and to whom we are very grateful. Nick Selby and Ian James of Melrose and Morgan, Andrew Davis, Josh Talmud, Tina Gaudoin, Ragi Dholakia, Megan Lichter, Frances Money, Melanie Solomou, Jess Leefe, Silvana Arzu, Faye MacGregor, Julia Murphy-Byske, Debbie Schogger, Simon Scarborough of Flemings Hotel, Tim Gow and Graham Penn have all in their different ways contributed greatly to the success of Primrose Bakery.

Our fantastic agent Charlotte Robertson, our editor Rowan Yapp of Square Peg, Jill Norman, Clare Alexander, Kyle Cathie, Peter and Pam White have all been especially helpful with the whole process of producing either our first or second book, both of which we are very proud of, and we are grateful to them all for their advice and guidance. For this book in particular we must thank Friederike Huber for her wonderful designs and ideas, Valerie Berry for her tireless and amazing cooking and help through the whole book photography process and to our photographer, Yuki Sugiura, for her truly beautiful photographs for both our books which have really managed to capture the spirit of Primrose Bakery. Martha's husband, Michael Heath, who we have already thanked on a personal level, has of course also helped us from the beginning of Primrose Bakery on a professional level with his unique and inspired illustrations for both our business and our books.

A final word of thanks must go to our customers – we have been privileged to make cakes for many different people and occasions since we started, and also to meet a huge variety of people who come to our shops, and we thank them all for their continued custom, support and feedback.

INDEX

Martha and Lisa both live in Primrose Hill, North London. Martha has two daughters and Lisa has two sons. They met when their children went to nursery school together fourteen years ago. Lisa is originally from New Zealand but settled in London twenty-one years ago. They set up Primrose Bakery seven years ago in Lisa's home kitchen. Lisa previously worked as a costume designer for films, and Martha worked in publishing.

www.primrosebakery.co.uk

For sweet treats on the go, download *The Primrose Bakery App* from iTunes